I have long believed that the heightened by the fact that no one impersonal and performance-driven culture now prefers emails, texts or Instagram. In an age when men cared about souls, letters were written. This is why we have the New Testament. My friend, Mike Milton, has provided an invaluable service to ministers by writing a series of letters to young seminarians about the ministry. I have read them and commend them to all pastors, future pastors and those in the pew being pastored. And I hope that this good endeavor by Dr Milton will motivate us to begin again to write letters. After all, such a treasure trove of pastoral wisdom comes to you "faithfully yours!" Take full advantage of this book.

Mike Ross,
Senior Pastor, Christ Covenant Church, Charlotte, North Carolina

Writing from years of experience, Mike Milton offers sage advice for theological students preparing for pastoral ministry. Written as a series of letters to a student, the personal warmth and pastoral overtones make this volume appealing and helpful.

Luder Whitlock,
Executive Director of CNL Charitable Foundation, Orlando, Florida

Mike Milton is a pastor to pastors. I know that because for more than twenty years he has counseled, encouraged, and inspired me. I am so grateful that now, in these letters, he has distilled that wisdom for a whole new generation of pastors.

George Grant,
Senior Pastor, Parish Presbyterian Church, Franklin, Tennessee

I did not anticipate the impact Mike Milton's Letters would have on me. As I read them I keep thinking here is a modern version of C.H. Spurgeon's *Lectures To My Students.* Mikes letters are warm, thoughtful, and practical. They should be read by every pastor, those studying for ministry, and those who care for ministers. We will use this book in our theological training at Erskine Seminary.

Paul D. Kooistra,
President, Erskine College and Seminary, Due West, South Carolina

Dr Milton reflects John Calvin's deep concern that pastors should serve with a heart warmed by the love of God for his people. Calvin wrote: "No one will ever be a good pastor, unless he shows himself to be a father to the Church that is committed to him." With this same passion Dr Milton calls young pastoral candidates to understand, and feel, the Good Shepherd's love for his flock so as to serve from that enduring passion. With wisdom, and many practical examples from his own blessed ministry, Milton quickens the minds and warms the hearts of all who would serve Christ's Church. While his letters are directed to young pastors and seminarians, they contain a timeless message – a message which warmed even this old pastor's heart.

Thomas D. Hawkes,
Senior Pastor, Uptown Church, Charlotte, North Carolina

This book is nectar. It is full of rich insights and helpful suggestions that cannot possibly fail to bless the reader and enrich his/her soul. All who take time to read it will be blessed and motivated in their service for Christ. My advice is: buy it and read it often.

Tom Holland,
Director of Biblical Research,
Wales Evangelical School of Theology, Bridgend, Wales

The
SECRET
LIFE
of a
PASTOR

The
SECRET
LIFE
of a
PASTOR

(and other intimate letters on ministry)

MICHAEL A. MILTON

CHRISTIAN
FOCUS

paperback ISBN 978-1-78191-596-7
epub ISBN 978-1-78181-597-4
mobi ISBN 978-1-78191-598-1

Published in 2015
by
Christian Focus Publications Ltd.
Geanies House, Fearn, Ross-shire,
IV20 1TW, Scotland, UK

www.christianfocus.com

Cover design by Daniel van Straaten

Printed by Bell and Bain, Glasgow

Contents

Dedicated to all of my students at Knox Theological Seminary, Erskine Theological Seminary, Reformed Theological Seminary, and the United States Army Chaplain Center and School. And always with love to my wife, Mae.

Acknowledgements

I have heard that some call the sermon – and I would say the pastoral sermon is this – 'the speaking of the Word of God in response to the dialogue of our daily lives.' In other words, preaching is not merely one's exegesis demonstrated for any who might listen; it is exegesis and exposition in the consecrated service to God's sacred community, the church.

Thinking of that definition helps me to see that the pastoral letters to seminary students in this book are attempts to teach God's Word on ministry in response to the dialogue of a larger community. These letters, it is my hope, are pastoral acts in the service of the church, but they were also shaped by the church. Just as a congregation shapes a pastor, so, also, the minister in the classroom – that is, a seminary professor – is formed and informed by students, colleagues, supporters, and practicing pastors.

In light of this, I want to recognize my students from Knox Theological Seminary in Fort Lauderdale; Erskine Theological Seminary in Due West, South Carolina; Reformed Theological Seminary at Charlotte and Orlando – and later, as chancellor, the entire RTS system of campuses – and the United States Army Chaplain Center and School, Fort Jackson, South Carolina. Each experience with the Masters of Divinity students, the

Doctor of Ministry students, and in the Army School's advanced chaplain courses has brought (and continues to bring) more insight into the study of the pastoral ministry. You are the community that has brought about these letters. Thank you. This book has also been written in the context of the wisdom of faculty colleagues in all of the institutions mentioned.

There are those who specifically contributed to these letters who should be recognized: Dr Rebecca Rine, who provides expert editorial assistance and consistently sound advice to me (on this project and others); Dr George Grant, who has been a (long-distance, but *never* absent) pastor and a true friend to me (and who was, once, one of my doctoral students); and Willie and Malcolm and all of our friends at Christian Focus Publications in Scotland. Thank you for waiting on this manuscript while I recovered. I thank, also, the model of pastoral ministry in my own life who continues in the ministry now into his eighth decade of life: my home church pastor, the Rev. Robert E. Baxter.

Finally, I thank my faithful wife, Mae. She read each of these letters, providing suggestions along the way, but (as every pastor out there knows) she did much more than that – more than anyone could imagine. She literally nursed me to a more sustainable level of health, assisted by our son, John Michael. All of our children, and now, their own families, contributed their part to make me whole.

So, this book is written 'in response to the dialogue of our daily lives'. But any errors that remain are all my own.

The living Lord Jesus Christ meets me daily in the power of the Father and the Spirit. His voice is the most powerful and influential voice of all. He is the One we aim to preach.

Mike Milton

Introduction

The book that you are holding represents pastoral letters that I composed to my students across the years, as I've had the opportunity to teach in seminaries. Vocational education for the ministry happens not only in formal classroom settings, but – perhaps, most effectively – in informal, intimate surroundings. In the world of emails and text-messages and other expressions of mass communication and social media the simple letter from one person to another – or from mentor to protégé, professor to students – has become all the more meaningful. Far from being anachronistic, I believe the unassuming, humble little epistle just may be on a rebound.

The more technologically dependent we are, the less authentically intimate we have become. Think about it: if we are, by necessity of storage space, destined to delete our quick, snappy communication trail every 120 days (a recommendation for many businesses), future historians will look back and find that there is a great gap in 'lower history' from the end of the twentieth century into the twenty-first. Now more than ever, I value the feel of a good fountain pen in my fingers, the flow of ink on a page of natural fibers, and the deeply humanizing experience of composing a letter. It is not that I am a Luddite or, for that matter, a snobby literary purist (I may or may not be; but in any case, most of these letters were first composed using email or another modern communication technique), but that the experience of teaching – and, therefore, learning – through letter-writing brings together various important features associated with the purer forms: a free-flowing mind-to-page composition, expressiveness in thought, language that speaks from the heart, and a constant concern for the one addressed. Student-centered teaching never met a better friend than a letter.

In my personal correspondence, I have sought to address things that are real in the life of pastors. What I have found is that everything that I write for students applies equally for seasoned pastors who have been in the ministry for many decades. I also believe that the content of these letters, which I seek to ground in an exclusively biblical foundation of thought, is apropos for non-clergy as well. We all shepherd others in one way or the other: parent to child, supervisor to subordinate, and even husband to wife and friend to friend. That said, these letters are especially focused on pastoral students and their particular situation and vocabulary. But this is not to say that others will not see themselves in these pages.

I believe that these letters – written with intimate care for the recipients, and authentically addressed to a real time and place and people – can be effective in the spiritual formation of pastors. Thus, I trust that as you would 'take and read' – to the degree that these letters adequately transmit the sacred Word of God – your soul will be shaped, your mind cultivated, and your heart inspired for the ministry that God has given you.

As each singular letter was written to a particular group of students at a particular time, the letters vary in length, language, and, at times, in tone. There is no cookie-cutter approach to mentoring, and the variations in the letters reflect this.

The common denominator in all of the published letters is the author's desire to lead future pastors and other church leaders in surrendering their identities, ambitions, and plans to the supreme Mentor, our Lord Jesus Christ. As James Houston reminded us so well in his book *The Mentor Life*, we can only learn what it is to be truly human when our lives are centered in His. If these letters help, in some way, to cultivate His life in you, then this book will have met its intended purpose.

I invite you, therefore, to take and read. And teach others, also.

M.A.M.
Fourth Sunday in Advent 2014

And you show that you are a letter from Christ delivered by us, written not with ink but with the Spirit of the living God, not on tablets of stone but on tablets of human hearts.

—St Paul, Second Corinthians 3:3

1

EXPECTATIONS ABOUT YOUR SEMINARY EXPERIENCE

Dearest Students in the Son of God,

Someone once said to me, 'Seminary never prepared me for what I faced in the ministry.' In his case the minister had been trained at a very sound seminary, so I wondered what he meant. I never felt that way about my own seminary (which was not Reformed Theological Seminary, but another biblically-sound seminary). What I learned was that this man was lamenting his situation out of a different set of expectations for ministerial education and preparation. And in this sense, I would argue that one should know the right purpose of a seminary education.

Your seminary is literally a seedbed for pastors (and for missionaries and others, but primarily, by virtue of the RTS charter, we are about training future pastors). Seminary must be seen in a more comprehensive way than merely by what you receive in the classroom. Of course, bringing that about will involve initiative by the seminary administration and faculty as well as enterprise by each student and cooperation with a local church. When this matrix of learning centers is brought together and seen as 'my seminary experience', then it should provide most (but not all) of the training one needs to begin pastoral practice according to the Scriptures.

Think of how seminary is similar to a medical school. Medical schools do not necessarily provide internships and residencies. They teach anatomy, they teach physiology, they teach the basics of medicine. In a similar way, a seminary provides the future pastor with grounding in the Word of God through Old and New Testament studies. The future pastor immerses himself in the Biblical languages because he will yet stand between God and men and women, boys and girls, with the Word of God. He will be the primary interpreter and expositor of the Word for the flock (within a plurality of eldership, but nevertheless the pastor is given this enormous role).

Since the pastor will be the repository of the sacred stories of God's dealing with the church, he must be grounded in church history. Because he is the caretaker of the hymnody and liturgy of the church he should be well taught in the theology of the worshipping life of the church. Among these and other things the seminary will teach the student about role relationships in the church and Biblical solutions for peacemaking.

In medical school, the study of anatomy alone cannot prepare a physician to begin his practice, so we must not suppose that the study of theology alone will prepare a man to practice as a pastor. He needs internships and he needs residency under a master. It is here that the student and the seminary and the church must seek ways to accomplish this critical component of pastoral preparation. While a student at a seminary will have to go through many hours of practical training, this cannot replace the week-to-week cycle of life in a local church.

A student in seminary needs to walk behind a senior pastor as he goes through his week. The student needs to see the pastor's work in staff meetings and in dealing with issues involving the administration of parish life. He needs to learn when he is with the pastor in deacon, session, or vestry meetings and how he governs through plurality and in meetings with others who are church leaders. Thus through sermon preparation, funerals, weddings and vigils with families waiting for loved ones to die, the future minister of the gospel completes his seminary preparation.

So, dear student, this is your residency. It will be as important as your theological training. There is no room to speak of one being more important than the other for an effective ministry in the future. Paul wrote the Pastoral Epistles and in them we find theological concepts and pastoral-theological implementation and pastoral approach to problems in the church. And so concept and praxis must be wed together in your education.

Therefore, soak up the glorious teaching you are receiving. Enjoy the relationships with your professors and with other students. Those days are meant to prepare you for a lifetime of ministry. But alongside your studies you must initiate a program of residency in which the theology gets its legs. Or as I have put it on several occasions, the funnel of ministry is filled with the entire theological encyclopedia. At the narrow end is a little girl in your congregation who is struggling with her faith, or an elder who is unhappy with your direction in evangelism, or a widow who is in pain as she approaches her first Christmas without her mate of fifty years. And there you are: their pastor. You are the one they look to for a word from God. At those moments, at the narrow end of the funnel, it must all come together. And to do that in your ministry you will need to have been well prepared.

(I have not even touched upon your devotional life! I will save that for another letter.)

I believe that if you follow this approach, dear students, you will never look back and say, 'Seminary did not prepare me for the ministry.' Indeed, you will be blessed by your investment and prepared for a lifetime of ministry.

Commending you to Christ and the Gospel of Grace, I am

Your servant,
Mike Milton.

❧2❧

ORIGINAL LANGUAGES

My dearest pastoral students in Christ,

A feature of the commencement of your seminary life at our graduate school here at Reformed Theological Seminary is your initial entry into one of the most challenging of classes: *the study of the original languages, Greek and Hebrew.* In fact, as I write, many first year students are in our 'Beginner Greek' modular courses scattered across our campus system. As they told me in boot camp, so I will tell you: 'It will get better!' Or will it? Can it?

Beyond the jests (that hide the pain!) there is a truth: *the study of the original languages chosen by God to reveal His plan of redemption to us is a marvelous opportunity afforded to only a few in the church.* You have been chosen!

Now, you may not be necessarily embracing your *divine election unto Greek* right now, as you have to learn to decline nouns and conjugate verbs and memorize all sorts of grammatical paradigms, not to mention vocabulary. Yet you must never forget this: 'Everyone to whom much was given, of him much will be required, and from him to whom they entrusted much, they will demand the more' (Luke 12:48).

First, I want you to think about how much is given to you in the study of the original languages. You have, as I have said, the opportunity that very few other believers in the world have: to study the inerrant and infallible Word of the living God in the original languages of the Bible. I will never forget the moment when I stood in class and read John 1:1 in the original Greek.

Every time that I see my retired Greek professor (Dr George W. Knight III), I bow down to him and kiss his ring! He always winces, draws his hand back, and tells me, 'Mike, get up from there, boy!' I do, of course, but then I tell him, 'Sir, if it were not for you I would not been able to read the New Testament in the language God chose. I could not have preached having done my own exegesis and study of the text in the original. It is such an honor.' And it is.

Pastors who have studied the original languages are able to go into the Word of God and exegete the sacred text, to dive deeper, and to gather richer expositions from the pool of truth and bring out pearls of eternal life to adorn their people, within the pulpit! What a wonderful honor and what an incredible pleasure. This is being given to you because you have been called to preach the unsearchable riches of Jesus Christ and you have made what I believe is a wise decision to come to RTS to prepare to undertake that solemn vocation. I thank God that we, with other fine but fewer seminaries than before, remain committed to the study of the original languages as a foundation for all pastoral studies. It is truly a gift.

Second, I want you to think about how much is required of you in the study of the original languages. The requirement that you have before the Lord is, first, to take the studies very seriously. Be as diligent in your study of the languages as you are in any other class. Don't think, 'If I can just slide through this, then I can get on with real seminary studies!' No! The languages are the bedrock of the rest of the course (the capstone, in my opinion, is pastoral theology, which is designed to integrate all other studies into the narrow field of application, according to Scripture, in the lives of human beings). On the foundation of the study of Greek and Hebrew, the other branches of the theological encyclopedia, such as biblical studies, systematic theology, apologetics, pastoral counseling, church history, pastoral leadership, and more, may be then surveyed.

Second, you have the requirement to approach your study with much prayer. Do not slip into the mindset that the study of languages is merely mechanical or perfunctory. Don't go about the learning of the languages as if you are learning a mathematical equation, soon to be forgotten and of no real practical necessity. No, my dearly beloved, you are learning the inerrant and infallible Word of God in the original languages and nothing could be more deeply spiritual.

Third, study with a heart of gratitude. You have a requirement to be one who comes to the Lord and says, 'Thank you, Lord Jesus, for allowing me to study your Word in the original languages. Help me, Heavenly Father, to be able to take your Word out into the world.' This is your requirement as you enter Greek or Hebrew this year: diligence, prayer and gratitude.

Maybe you'll never go to your New Testament or Old Testament professor in future years and kiss his ring! That is a bit over-the-top I admit (but I also like to have fun with my friend!). What you may want to do is to say 'thank you' to those rare ministers of Christ who have invested a lifetime in the study and cultivation of the original languages of the Holy Bible. They are noble shepherds with a unique task in the Father's fields. Let us honor them well.

My son grew up hearing his father 'pre-preach' his messages every Saturday night in our family devotions. As a result our son has grown-up hearing the Word of God, not only daily in morning and evening devotions, but also exposited in Saturday night sermons. Then, he would get it again on Sunday morning and Sunday night! More than that, we often speak much of God's Word in our home as I wrestle with a passage out loud with my family. As a result, I tell him all the time, 'You have been given an opportunity that few other believers have: and that is to have the Word in your home and to have never known a day where you didn't know of the name Jesus.' In a similar way, I want to speak to you, our sons and daughters in Christ, who are taking the biblical languages this semester. I want to tell you, you have a great privilege. You also now have a great responsibility.

I pause to pray for our seminary as we get ready to enter a new year of preparing gospel preachers, pastors, missionaries, counselors, and other servants who will open up the Word of God and speak His truth to the world. May the Holy Spirit come down and anoint all of our work – even our Greek and Hebrew modular classes!

I desire to be, now and always,
Yours Faithfully,
Mike Milton.

3

BROKEN CISTERNS: A WORD OF COUNSEL ON THE MATTER OF PASTORAL SELF CARE

Dear Students in the Gospel Ministry,

There is an Old Testament passage to which I would draw your attention as I ask you to think of your future ministries. It is a warning that was given to the people of Israel: 'For my people have committed two evils: they have forsaken me, the fountain of living waters, and hewed out cisterns for themselves, broken cisterns that can hold no water' (Jer. 2:13).

The ancient people of God knew a basic fact of life – man must have water to live. The soul is no different from the body. This is the underlying truth of the metaphor of water and cisterns in Jeremiah 2. Thus, we need spiritual water to live as human beings, and in the fullest revelation of Scripture, Jesus Christ, the Son of God, is the living water. Nothing else, no one else, can satisfy the human soul. But you know that already. You are mature believers. You are pastors-in-training. You know that Jesus said that whoever drank of his water would never thirst again (John 4:14).

I want to tell you that human nature has not changed from the time that Jeremiah warned the culturally sophisticated Hebrews, living in Jerusalem, worshipping at the grand and glorious House of God, that they had committed two evils that would bring about a spiritual disease, which if not remedied, would result in death. And the tendencies of those people reoccur with our people. And they reoccur with us as pastors too. We commit two evils that bring about spiritual drought. This is the real reason why I write to you at this time.

As a pastor, each of you will be giving constantly to your people your very life. There will be ongoing demands upon your soul. On Monday night there is a session meeting and the elders will go to work the next day, leaving you to work out what was discussed. You will live with the challenge of the difficult decision to cut the budget for world missions. You will wake up the next day and the pain left by toxic words from an irritated colleague will still be hurting. But you won't have time to nurse your wounds. Mrs Galloway is coming in early to give her opinion about the children's Christmas pageant that has been changed from the way it has been done since she was a little girl. She is eighty-two now. But you know that beneath her concern there is a widow still grieving over the loss of Mr Galloway. And her son, Bill, was killed in Vietnam. So you will suffer through the presenting issues – and try to figure out how to help her and the children's director who defends her changes in the play as being best for the parents and children – in order to get to the real issues.

Then, you will meet with the administrator to work through some worn-carpet issues in the narthex, and after that you go to the Lion's Club to give the invocation. You will sit with the incoming chairman for this year, who is also one of your deacons. You are glad for him, even though you know that doing one more thing is only another example of the hyperactivity in church functions that seems to be taking him away from a troubled marriage. You have been praying about that, but you are not sure if you should say anything about it today.

After the lunch at the Lion's Club, you will have coffee with a campus minister who is seeking financial support. Your church has no more money designated for mission, but you will help him network with an elder you know from First Church, and they may have funds. The Lord knows that the college needs him there. And so will your daughter – she is going to the college next year!

After coffee, you hope to find time to work on the Wednesday night Bible study and maybe even return to the Sunday sermon. But then again you will not likely get to them if Mr Bryant's heart surgery takes longer than expected. You could be there throughout the afternoon. In a way, you want to be there for that length of time because Mr Bryant's adult son will be there. Reconciliation is something that you have been praying for since the young man moved in with his girlfriend. It will be tense, but it is the right place to be.

Your youngest daughter has a dance recital tonight, and your wife wants to eat out before the recital and maybe get ice cream with another family from the dance school afterwards. You want to as well. But you know that there is a men's study the next morning, and you will need to prepare for it. As you crawl through the oncoming list of demands – good, bad, and otherwise – you begin to feel really thirsty. It is then that the real test comes.

And on it goes. I am not trying to scare you, but this is life in the ministry. It is not the ministry every day, but it is what some days will be like. Many days, in fact. And if you don't watch out you will often only be going to the well in order to give spiritual water to others. Unless you replenish your own soul at the well, you will become dry.

It will start with *physical* signs of spiritual dehydration: fatigue that you can't shake off, headaches, waking up too early, not being able to go back to sleep, a change in appetite, and increased sickness.

You will sense it *emotionally*: feeling blue, increased frustration and even hostility, harder to concentrate, apathy and a desire to withdraw from others, and discord at home. At work, if you could see it, you would observe a loss of efficiency, increased frustration with others in the ministry team, decreased satisfaction with your vocation, and no more dreaming about what could be.

Spiritually, you begin to experience disappointment with God. You start to wonder if God cares for you, even as you preach to others, mechanically, about His love. Your devotional practices change. Reading, prayer, personal worship and even corporate worship do not seem real anymore. So what do you do? You exchange the invitation to come closer to Jesus Christ, the living Water who would flood your soul with His presence and power, for more work.

Others bring you cisterns that will surely capture some water for you. But there is no replacement for the presence of God Himself, practiced in silence, in Christian meditation, and in prayer. That is returning to God, counteracting the first evil of departing from Him. And the second is returning to His Word, and living out of His Word, which overcomes the second evil of drinking at other wells.

The pressing demands of shepherding a flock of Christ will still be there. But you will be whole, filled, refreshed, and able to minister out of the reservoir of your union in Christ.

You will need this along the way. And I was thinking about you today. So I commend you to Christ and to the Word of His grace, and know that I am,

Yours Faithfully,
Mike Milton.

❦4❦

THE SECRET LIFE OF A PASTOR

My beloved students in the pastoral ministry,

'What is the pastoral life really like?' the prospective seminary student asked me on a recent visit. 'I will tell you (I lean in and whisper). Would you like to know about the secret life of the pastor? Pull up a seat and let's talk.'

I began by going back to the day when I asked such questions myself. The illumined ones know the truth: it is not what so many think. The keys of the kingdom are not yours any more than they are the deacon's or the custodian's. The life of a pastor is centered not in position, but in passion – a passion that costs.

I remember my old mentor, Dr D. James Kennedy, telling me that a pastor must love God, God's Word, and God's People. I believe his admonition of these simple and profound intuitive desires came from a singular passion stirred in the heart of the pastor by God Himself. These three 'loves' cannot be manufactured by man or instilled by a seminary. This is altogether the incomparable work of God in the human soul. However, these 'three loves' can – no, must – be stirred, kindled and expanded for even more productive ministry through the ordinary means of grace given to a pastor.

Consider 1 Thessalonians 2, a passage from the mind and heart of Paul – one passage that has meant so much to me in every station of my pastoral ministry.[1] We think of this peerless

---

1. 'For you yourselves know, brothers, that our coming to you was not in vain. But though we had already suffered and been shamefully treated at Philippi, as you know, we had boldness in our God to declare to you the gospel of God in the midst of much conflict. For our appeal does not spring from error or impurity or any attempt to deceive, but just as we have been approved by God to be entrusted with the gospel, so we speak, not to please man, but to please God who tests our hearts. For we never came with words of flattery, as you know, nor with a pretext for greed – God is witness. Nor did we seek glory from people, whether from you or from others, though we could have made demands as apostles of Christ. But we were gentle among you, like a nursing mother taking care of her own children. So, being affectionately desirous of you, we were ready to share with you not only the gospel of God but also our own selves, because you had become very dear to us.

'For you remember, brothers, our labor and toil: we worked night and day, that we might not be a burden to any of you, while we proclaimed to you the gospel of God. You are witnesses, and God also, how holy and righteous and blameless was our conduct toward you believers. For you know how, like a father with his children, we exhorted each one of you and encouraged you and charged you to walk in a manner worthy of God, who calls you into his own kingdom and glory.

'And we also thank God constantly for this, that when you received the word of God, which you heard from us, you accepted it not as the word of men but as what it really is, the word of God, which is at work in you believers. For you, brothers, became imitators of the churches of God in Christ Jesus that are in Judea. For you suffered the same things from your own countrymen as they did from the Jews, who killed both the Lord Jesus and the prophets, and drove us out, and displease God and oppose all mankind by hindering us from speaking to the Gentiles that they might be saved – so as always to fill up the measure of their sins. But wrath has come upon them at last!

'But since we were torn away from you, brothers, for a short time, in person not in heart, we endeavored the more eagerly and with great desire to see you face

genius and tireless teacher of truth as the great apostle, evangelist, missionary and ambassador of the gospel to the Gentiles, and yet here, and in some other places in his writings, we come face to face with one of the greatest pastors of all time. Oh what a portrait of a true, Christ-like, good shepherd is here painted by Paul's heart disclosed and open for all to see! What do we learn about the 'secret life' – the passionate life – of a pastor of Christ's flock? The illuminati are those who simply, purposely, patiently and carefully read the ink of the Holy Spirit in the scribbling of Paul's pen.

A Broken Heart

Paul's words in seeking to communicate his heart to the Thessalonians not only convey his love for them, but also demonstrate to us that the pastorate is risky work, because you risk your heart. 'It is dirty work,' O. Palmer Robertson said of those who are compared to sheep tenders by Jesus. Quite. When you preach the Word publicly and privately; when you bring the Word in the Bread and the Cup to the saints, when you are there at their physical and spiritual births, and when you pour the covenantal waters of baptism over the dear heads of these people, I assure you that you will never be the same.

'Is it like being in love with a girl, then? Is it like being away from the one you love? Is that the pain that Paul speaks of when he writes about being "torn away from you"?' It is that, and more. It is being in love with the church, I say. It is having your heart filled and overflowing with the celestial-earthly beauty of what Christ is doing in human souls.

'But aren't they ornery creatures, these sheep?' Yes, and so are you! Yet the most difficult child is still loved by the tender-

---

to face, because we wanted to come to you – I, Paul, again and again – but Satan hindered us. For what is our hope or joy or crown of boasting before our Lord Jesus at His coming? Is it not you? For you are our glory and joy' (1 Thess. 2).

hearted mother. God loves those for whom Christ died, and you will too if you minister in the power of the Spirit (and not the flesh). The saints of God, however, may not understand that your love is greater than their insults or indifference or waywardness or criticisms.

'But,' the applicant continues, 'I have heard it said that there are "divine subtractions"!' No, I say. There are problem-people, but if there were not, would there be a need for a pastor? I tell you that the greatest heartache and regrets I have are not in the time invested in the 'lovable saints', but in protecting myself from the 'unintentional dragons'. I would rather, now, spend more time with them than any other. Their nasty e-mails and their thoughtless barbs were so often the cloaked cries of wounded spirits. And I withdrew. Oh how I would go back a thousand times to hold them until the stiffness went away.

Just ask a pastor who is loved and then, through one circumstance or another, is removed from the saints. He will tell you that his heart has been torn in two. But here is the thing, my beloved: this is your life as a pastor. You will have a broken heart. To love is to be hurt, they say. To open your life to others is to open your heart to brokenness. Christ had a broken heart like no other pastor (and He is the chief pastoral model in all of Scripture). Think of His heart broken as He wept at the funeral of His friend Lazarus, or as He wept over the inhabitants of Jerusalem who would turn against Him. He was a man of sorrows, acquainted with grief. Yet through this broken heart He comes to us as One who knows our broken hearts. So God breaks your heart as a pastor in order that you will love even more. For God does not want shepherds who do not love, who do not weep, who cannot feel the pain of separation from the flock. 'Love God, Love God's Word, and Love God's People,' Dr Kennedy said, and I cannot but become very emotional as

31

I recall that charge to me and then read these words of Paul's as I write to you, my beloved.

An Unexpected Journey

Note that Paul said that 'we wanted to come to you' but had been 'torn away'. Paul had intended to come to them. Initially he did not want to write an epistle to them. Instead he had wanted to bring the gospel to them personally. Yet his ministry there, and in other places, was always being re-routed because of the devil's opposition (only a mere secondary cause in the glorious redemptive plan of God) or even in some cases (no in all cases, even in this case) sovereignly diverted by the Holy Spirit to accomplish God's purposes in the world at exactly the perfect time. But oh how costly such diversions are to the soul of the minister of Christ!

There would be no pain, of course, if there were no love. Ask the pastor who has loved a flock and expected to minister to that congregation for the rest of his life, only to discover that his plan, a good plan, was not God's? Was Paul's desire to go to Asia wrong? Of course not. Yet the Holy Spirit forbade him to go in order that he would head westward to bring the gospel of life to Lydia and her European spiritual progeny. What of Paul's journey from Corinth to Jerusalem after he declared that he would never preach again to the Jews? Yet he was redirected to return to the Jews to preach Christ to them.

The old Methodists took a vow of itinerary, realizing that they would be sent wherever Bishop Asbury would decide. So, too, do you, in a way, take such a vow when you surrender to gospel ministry. The Bishop of your soul, the Head of the Church, may send you to places that you do not want to go to. Yet His kingdom vision is what guides you; not your own. Thus the ministry is, as it was to Pastor Paul, a most unexpected journey. The sooner you come to terms with this vow of love the sooner you will be contented in God's service, and trust that unexpected journeys are never unexpected to God.

A Diabolical Opposition

If you have never seen the reality of Satanic activity, you need not go to an ancient animistic culture in a third world country, or to a pagan pageantry in a foggy, green jungle, or to an idolatrous village along the Ganges, in order to see it; you have only to do the work of the Lord with zeal where you are. Satan sought to disrupt the relationship of Paul and the Thessalonians. Why? The answer to that question is no more remote than the very vision of the Great Commission of Jesus Christ!

In the pastoral ministry, the saints grow by the preaching of the Word, by the prayers, by the Scripture reading, by the singing of the psalms and hymns of faith, by pastoral visitation, and by the ministry of presence – the faithful, week-in and week-out pointing to Jesus of Nazareth. All regular pastoral work leads to a growth in the kingdom (too often unnoticed by even the pastor) as faith is strengthened and then passed from generation to generation.

But fear not, oh messenger of Christ! He who overcame the devil in the wilderness will guard you in such seasons of devilish attack. He who was comforted by heavenly angels in the desolate place after an obedience in the desert which Moses and the children of Israel could not accomplish, and which you and I cannot accomplish without Him, will send angels to succor you. Paul's heart-wounds, after being diverted by the devil, become the sacred time of writing this very letter, which still instructs us today. Thus will Christ always deliver His pastors unto everlasting life, even should the devil and the world bring martyrdom to them! We live under the motif of the Cross and the Empty

Tomb. This is the ground on which we conduct our ministry to the world.

An Others-Centered Identity

Paul asks, 'For what is our hope or joy or crown of boasting before our Lord Jesus at his coming?' This question had already been answered in his heart. Paul writes that his hope, joy and crown of boasting in 'you' at Christ's coming has become his very identity.

The pastorate is not a job or a career like so many. It is, rather, very similar to the identity of a physician of the body. The physician's work flows from his identity. He is 'Doctor so and so'. He cannot separate himself from his healing arts and his availability to the wounded community. He is a doctor of the body whether he is a spectator at a high school football game or whether he is in his lab coat in his office. He is and must always be a doctor.

Thus, the physician of the soul is one whose identity is totally tied to a sacred encounter with the Christ who calls, and with the people that he is called to serve with his very life. So, as Paul poses this rhetorical question (a question that Paul wanted to answer so that he would bring joy into the hearts of his spiritual children, the Thessalonians), so we who are pastors join with the *Apostle of the Heart Set Free*[2] and declare that our identity also is in Christ and is with His church, the blessed redeemed of God. Our identity is others-centered.

A Present Joy in a Future Hope

In a similar and climactic way, Paul links the hope and the joy and the rejoicing, or boasting, not only in the saints of God,

---

2. This was the title of a book on the Apostle Paul by F.F. Bruce, the well-known British biblical scholar.

but also in a day when his ministry will be completed: at the parousia of Jesus. There, in that day, when as Fanny Crosby wrote in her hymn, there will be 'souls safe in the arms of Jesus', Paul will know the fully ripened fruit of his pastoral ministry. And so will you!

Your pastorate is not judged only by the number of those who come to Christ, or are healed of soul, or commit to the Kingdom of Jesus in your lifetime, but who multiply that conversion, that healing, that Kingdom work, by sharing their faith through the years, through their familial and their spiritual descendants. They, all of them, are yours (that is, they are Christ's), in the sense that you will see how powerful Christ is with so weak a worker as yourself.

You will see how God multiplied ministry even though your heart was broken as you were 'run out' of one pastorate only to find a new love in another pastorate (though you never stopped loving the saints in the previous pastorate; for the saints in all the churches we serve are like flowers we gather from the several parts of the fields of Christ that we serve; flowers which are preserved for us through all the days of our lives, and even unto eternity). This is our hope and our joy and our crown – our people safe in the arms of the true Shepherd.

But of course that is where we shall also be, safe in His arms. The shepherd's heart healed, his journey completed, all opposition thwarted (and used to bring him home), and his identity absorbed with the One he followed, as the pastor joins with the saints and proceeds towards the Lamb's throne, and that which was preached for so long and with so many tears and trials is now the hope fulfilled. And the pastor's tears are wiped away by God Himself.

Dearest students in the gospel of grace, and especially those of you called by Christ to shepherd His flock, read St Paul – read his pastor's heart in his pastoral words – and be comforted by the Holy Spirit. Then go and love God, love God's Word, and love God's saints. There is no other work like it in this world. And it will end in another world that is already on its way.

Yours Faithfully,
Mike Milton.

5

HEALERS, NOT DOCTORS

Dear Students,

We cared so much for you that we were pleased to share with you not only the gospel of God but also our own lives, because you had become very dear to us (1 Thess. 2:8).

There is a bad idea out there which says that the truly effective pastor should either be a free-wheeling entrepreneurial sort who fits right in with the trendy troupe in Silicon Valley, or a prophet-like figure who distantly removes himself from the everyday affairs of people to give himself to isolated, devout study, and then comes out of his 'pastor cave' to give forth the Word, generally in rather dour and somber tones, from his time in the 'heavenlies'.

Both of these ideas are stereotypes, and polarized ones at that! Yet there is a way that we, particularly in what I refer to as 'the post seminary stress syndrome' (not yet recognized by the American Psychological Association), can fall into these traps.

As a freshly minted MDIV, out to teach systematic theology (that is to teach my professor's entire systematic theology) in eight lessons, and plant a church and school, and save the world (and wondering why no one really saw the genius in me that I saw), I hit the wall. No one knew it, I guess. Maybe if you talked to some laity after it happened, they would say they saw it coming. Maybe my wife will tell you about it. For it was there. While no one could ever accuse this Martyn Lloyd-Jones-want-to-be (whose memory and ministry I cherish) of fitting into Silicon Valley, I did somewhat fit the part of a prophet-in-waiting.

The problem with all of these things is that it misses the essential mark of the very heart of St Paul: a gentle man who gave the gospel and his very life to his people out of his deep love. He was a man who did not use his authority (1 Thessalonians 2:7, '…though we could have made demands as apostles of Christ') but was like a nursing mother among the people, whom the Apostle considered his own children ('But we were gentle among you, like a nursing mother taking care of her own children'). He was a gentle, maternal-like figure ready to give his own life to the congregation, a man who was feeding on Christ from within his own affectionate heart. This marked his ministry. And do you think they loved him?

I have a theory, tested only on myself and those assistants I have mentored, that congregations shape pastors as much as does the seminary. We at RTS do the work of preparing you, like a medical school prepares a physician, but it is at the bedside of a sick child that a fledgling physician learns to apply his study of diagnosis with love. It is in the eyes of the child looking to him for hope, that the doctor becomes a healer. We need more healers and fewer doctors. It is in the eyes of a widower, who is looking to you for answers, that you must locate the love of God in your life to give to him. It is during those moments, as much as in the study or in considering the latest sociological trends, that you become a pastor. We need more who seek to be healers and true physicians of the soul in the pulpit and the parish and fewer who aspire to be prophets and entrepreneurs.

Here is what I want to say to you, dearest pastoral students: minister with passion, out of the love you received in the Lord Jesus Christ, and love the flock of God out of the overflow of love that you have known from Jesus in your life. And you will say of your people what Paul said of his: '…you had become very dear to us.' Be sure, also, that they will say that of you as well.

Yours Faithfully,
Mike Milton.

6

YOU ARE THE LIVING LEGACY OF THOSE WHO HAVE GONE BEFORE: ANOTHER MOTIVATION TO GO THE DISTANCE IN MINISTRY

Dearest Students in the Gospel Ministry,

I want to tell you a story about myself and then ask something of you. But first let me give you a Scripture to start your studies with today: 'But as for you, continue in what you have learned and have firmly believed, knowing from whom you learned it and how from childhood you have been acquainted with the sacred writings, which are able to make you wise for salvation through faith in Christ Jesus' (2 Tim. 3:14-15).

I was orphaned as a child. My Aunt Eva adopted and reared me. At sixty-five years of age, never having had any children of her own and recently widowed, an eighteen-month-old baby was placed in her arms. I was the child. Aunt Eva reared me in a rural, poverty-stricken area of southeastern Louisiana, in the piney woods, on the border with Mississippi. She prayed for me every day. That is not hyperbole. She laid her hands on me and prayed for me. Years later, after I had gone through a 'prodigal journey' and then came to the Lord in repentance and faith, she was there. She had prayed me home.

When Mae and I married and God called me to preach, Eva went with us to seminary. She was there at my commissioning as a US Army Reserve chaplain. She was there when I founded a church and school in Overland Park, Kansas. At ninety-nine years of age, she lay dying. Before she left this world, she blessed our son, John Michael, who was then a baby. She thanked my wife for all she had done (to straighten me out!!) and to care for her. Then, she drew me near to her and whispered with the remaining strength she had, 'My son, keep up the good work of the Lord.' I will never forget that moment. She then slipped into the presence of the Lord she had worshiped for so long.

A few years ago, the late Dan Fogelberg, a great folk singer, composed and recorded a song about his father. He called it, 'Leader of the Band.' There is a line in that song that I love, that I sing along with, and that I always personalize (and others likely do so as well, because it is the key to the popularity of the song). The line is, 'I am the living legacy of the leader of the band.' I, too, know that I am only the living legacy of a woman of faith, my Aunt Eva. I am little more and nothing less than that. But because of her, because of her influence in my life, her love, her pattern of faith, I want to move forward in that same faith. I may stumble and I may fall, but in the toughest times that I may face, I want to sing that line again, 'I am the *living legacy* of … Aunt Eva.'

How about you? Who is the one who prayed for you, or whispered in the ear of your soul, 'Son, daughter, keep up the good work.'? When you sing, 'I am the living legacy', whose name do you mention? I raise this to encourage you to remember those who would cheer you on, as it were. Oh that you could think of those who helped you to this point! Oh that your heart could be stirred to go the distance as you begin a new spring semester, or, with some of you, conclude your seminary time and begin to think about a transition to ministry!

All of us should be moved by those who have gone before us, who have mentored us, who have loved us, and who have sacrificed so that we could be here today, serving the Lord. What an honor and privilege!

So, I say, 'Thanks, Lord. Thanks, Aunt Eva.' And I say to you, 'Continue in what you have learned and have firmly believed, knowing from whom you learned it' and dedicate your service to our Triune God and to those He gave you in this life. Then 'come hungry' each day to learn, to give, to soak up the blessings of our seminary camaraderie, and to be inspired and to inspire.

The Lord bless and keep you, and help you to become a legacy to cheer someone else on as well.

Yours Faithfully,
Mike Milton.

7

YOUR WIFE, YOUR CHILDREN
AND THE CHURCH

My dear Students and Beloved in Christ,

I want to talk to you about your wife, your children, your ministry and the church. What I want to say is, 'Be careful about the way you speak of the bride of Christ in your home.' No one will see what John Stott calls the 'ambiguity of the church' more than you will. What I mean is that as you preach and teach the glorious vision of the church with, for example, the superlatives that Paul uses of it in Ephesians, and as you speak, with Paul, of giving your life 'for the sake of the elect' (2 Tim. 2:10), you will do so with a church that is still on its way, that has not 'arrived' at its glorification yet!

Indeed, as you will preach about the glory of the church from the pulpit, you will see something quite different from what you do when you live with the church in the parish. You will preach your heart out concerning sin and its consequences only to have

Miss Mercurial lambast you at the front door about sipping water during one of your points and distracting her (I have had that one!). You will receive angry emails berating you for a grammatical mistake in a sermon in which your passion for the text belied your modest, country origins, a revelation that Mrs Propriety found 'out of decorum for the pulpit of our venerable church' (I have had that one too!). You will receive from the hands of another pastor, who happened to get an inkling of it, a circular letter calling you a 'catastrophe' because of your explicit preaching of the Reformed faith ('But you are a Reformed pastor...' I know, but...), and your insensitivity to other traditions which are more Biblical! When you observe that the circular is signed 'faithfully yours' by one of your officers, Mr Smith, who also wants you out of the church, it really hurts (I have had that one as well!). And when a parishioner says that your child is obviously getting too much sugar before church, and that he can recommend a good child psychologist or nutritionist, it gets a bit much (I have not had that one, but pretty close), and it is enough to send you packing and singing, 'I'll Fly Away.' Nevertheless that is the church too. It is the church composed of a people on their way, but who have not arrived yet.

The beatific vision of the glorious bride of Christ is there. But your theology of 'progressive' sanctification really kicks in when you compare the church of Ephesians with the church in Corinth, which is, of course, your church. They both are. But here is the thing: you will be tempted to bring only one of those visions home with you. And after a long session meeting in which you will be encouraged for your stand in the pulpit for the truth of God's Word and also in which one of your officers will blame the summer slump in giving on your latest sermon series (I have had that one!), which comment will you bring home and tell your wife?

Your wife will respond in the way a wife ought to respond: she will support you. This will comfort you, and so you go deeper. You tell her more. You tell her that the session meeting that night is only the tip of the iceberg. You tell her about Miss Mercurial and Mrs Propriety and Mr Smith. As you tell her, her blood boils. And you? You feel better. You are soothed by her defense, by her outrage at such behavior. Then she serves dinner, and since you enjoyed being gratified by her companionship in your pain, you now inform your children. Your teenage son is mortified by anyone daring to raise a negative word about his father (that one feels good!). But then your six-year-old daughter interrupts the session and asks, with a whimpering sound in her little voice, 'But Daddy, I thought they loved you and you loved them? Aren't we supposed to love each other, Daddy? Isn't that what you said last Sunday at church?' The table is quiet. And a little child shall lead them.

Be careful that you don't give your family only one side of the 'ambiguity', the progressive sanctification side. Remember: you are the pastor. And God would not call pastors unless there were sheep that needed a shepherd. If they were all following perfectly, none infected, none at risk of the wolf, none too close to the edge of the high and craggy cliff, then you would not have a calling. But they (and we) don't follow perfectly. They (and we) are infected. They (and we) are at risk. They (and we) are navigating treacherous cliffs in this life.

If you only tell your family about the ugly side of the church, then that is the opinion they will have of it. It is not that they are not smart enough or not spiritual enough to know the difference. It is only that the love and relationships of family will begin to color their view of the church.

And the truth is, you will return to the church the next day to counsel Miss Mercurial and then learn about the pain she is experiencing from being the perennial bridesmaid and the lost love of a romance that didn't work out too many years ago. You will learn about Mrs Propriety's dead husband, who was an alcoholic and an adulterer, and how she could never mourn for him and yet she thought she was supposed to. And you will discover that Mr Smith does indeed hate you. And he hates his wife, his employer, the last pastor, the postman, the grocer and anyone who comes into contact with him. And you will learn that his father abandoned him when he was a lad. You will discover the real issues beneath the presenting issues. And in many cases you will help pastor such people, and the session member who blamed you for a bad August giving period, to drink of the waters of grace. Some will follow. Some will not. But your wife and children will never know anything of what has been shared in these counseling sessions. They will be forever stuck with the vision of the ugly church that is hurting her husband and attacking their dad.

It is easier to complain to your family and murmur about the problem people than to speak of the healing that you are able to see over time. So be careful. You could cause callousness to develop in the souls of your family members. You could leave them with a burden that they were not intended to bear. Some children grow up and say, 'I have had enough of the church. Why would I want to get into something that hurt my family so much?' Or you will hear your wife tell you, 'I want out. I am tired of all of the criticism.'

What is the answer? 'Don't tell your wife anything?' No. Instead, be careful. Let her in on your challenges in the same way as a physician might let his wife in on a perplexing case that is before him. Ask your wife, and perhaps your children, to join you in prayer over the person, without giving a name. And then remember that person in family prayer and, as you see God's healing becoming evident, give thanks in family worship as well. In this way your wife and children are brought into your ministry, not positioned as enemies with others, hunkering down and waiting for an attack, or feeling defeated or victimized.

Of course there will be times when you will be attacked. There are times when it is not a sheep that is coming after you, but a wolf. In those times seek the wisdom of God on how to share the matter with your wife. I would not share it with my children until they were old enough to understand the deep matters of spiritual warfare (which some adult Christians don't understand!). And knowing the difference between a hurting lamb fighting back in the pain and a hateful wolf perching for attack will require a life of prayer, wisdom from on high, and often confidential counsel with other pastors and elders. Many times it will require 20/20 hindsight, which brings us back to not saying anything at all. 'But that will hurt me! I cannot be expected to keep things inside. I have to let it all out!' Well, it may hurt you. And you may end up carrying things to your grave. Or, you could carry them to the Savior!

I have managed large areas of responsibility of Fortune 500 companies, and packed 100-pound iron pipes on my back in the oil fields in the sweltering summer swamps of coastal Louisiana, but nothing I have ever done is as challenging as the pastorate. And nothing is more fulfilling. Why? Because this is your calling. Remember Paul's words: 'Therefore do not be ashamed of the testimony about our Lord, nor of me his prisoner, but share in suffering for the gospel by the power of God, who saved us and called us to a holy calling, not because of our works but because of his own purpose and grace, which he gave us in Christ Jesus before the ages began' (2 Tim. 1:8-9).

So let your wife and children hear you say: 'Therefore I endure everything for the sake of the elect, that they also may

obtain the salvation that is in Christ Jesus with eternal glory'
(2 Tim. 2:10). I am thinking about you, your families, and the
covenant children of our pastors who need to hear that their
daddies love the church, the church that needs pastors to bring
the healing of Christ to hurting sheep.

Yours Faithfully,
Mike Milton.

EQUIPPERS OF THE SAINTS

Dear Friends in Christ,

There are many bad ideas about the essential job description of the pastor. Yet in the Word of God there is zero ambiguity. In Ephesians 4:11-12, pastors and teachers, or pastor-teachers, the ordinary office of servant-leadership in the church, exist to 'equip the saints for the work of ministry'.

Is equipping the saints mentoring them so to engage in ministry tasks such as visiting the sick? Yes, it is. Is it teaching elders and deacons how to work out that basic biblical division of labor according to the Scriptures? Most certainly. Is it assisting in Vacation Bible School, helping the janitor clean up after a spill in the fellowship hall, or stretching a broom stick to knock down an old wasps' nest from the eaves of the sanctuary (all of which I have done and happily recommend as therapy for proud pastors)? Of course!

I believe that as servants of the church of Jesus Christ, we may find ourselves doing all of those things and many more.

And this is in some way living out our calling. But should we be making sure everyone is plugged in to one program or another, like the fraternity rush chairman (so they won't go to the 'in' church down the street)? Or is it being like a circus ringmaster who keeps the act going, keeps the plates spinning, for the benefit of more and more visitors and more and more activity? No. God forbid. You are not a rush chairman or a ringmaster. Neither are you an executive, a CEO, a coordinator, or a salesman. You are a pastor, the man chosen of God to equip the saints for the work of ministry. Only in the God-ordained role, in the Christ-commanded work, and through biblically revealed ways will you find your vocational satisfaction for the pastoral ministry. There is no other way.

Now, the work of ministry is plain in the Bible. It is, to borrow Lesslie Newbigin's famous and simple phrase, to 'fulfill God's purposes on earth'. The work of ministry is to be about the Great Commandment (to love one another) and the Great Commission (to baptize and make disciples of the nations and to teach them whatsoever Jesus commanded), in order to bring about the Great Consummation of a 'new heavens and a new earth'.

Thus, our people are to witness everywhere (Acts 8:4), and show mercy (Matt. 5:7), justice and the love of God to the world (Luke 11:42), and to bring gospel truth and the teaching of Christ to every area of life. The Kuyperian view that no single area of human existence is exempt from the Lordship of Jesus is the view of many in the Reformed faith, and I am convinced that it is the Bible's view. Thus the Great Commission of Matthew 28 and the Cultural Mandate of Genesis 1 remain the work of the church of Jesus Christ until He comes again. And because the nations are to be taught the Word, led to pray, and to receive the signs of salvation (baptism and the Lord's Supper), pastors will have a life-long work. This is what you will be equipping the saints to do. It is a glorious work and one that you are preparing for here in Seminary.

It is right that you prepare by studying the theology derived and systematized from the Word. It is good that you study the texts, in the original languages, of the Old and New Testaments. It is noble that you study the mighty acts of God in history, the mistakes, the councils, the trials, the joys of the church, and the faithfulness of God through it all in church history and that you begin to develop a historical theology. It is a blessing to study the application of theology in a distinctive pastoral theology so that you can address this glorious work through your preaching, leading in worship, counseling, training for evangelism and principles of servanthood (leadership).

But how does one go about this work? That is the question in the minds of many today. The answer is plain and without ambiguity or shadows of meaning. You are to equip the saints through word, sacrament and prayer. Rev. Terry Johnson of Independent Presbyterian Church in Savannah, Georgia, once told me that when he was called to that venerable congregation he wanted to ask a seasoned pastor how he might best serve Christ. He inquired of a good one: the late and deeply missed James Montgomery Boice, the former pastor of Tenth Presbyterian Church in Philadelphia. As I recall it, Dr Boice simply told him, 'Preach and pray.' 'That's your advice?' Dr Johnson might have asked, hoping for more insights. 'That's it,' Dr Boice would have replied.

When Jesus commissioned Peter, revealing to him that he was incapable of following without the divine love of Jesus in his poor heart, the Savior told him, 'Feed my sheep.' He said no more. 'That's it.' There could be no question about how. Peter, the apostle, Peter the evangelist, would shepherd the people of

God in Jerusalem and in Asia Minor and in Rome through the 'ordinary means of grace'.

'Preach and pray.' Give them Jesus in baptism. Show them Jesus in the Lord's Supper. Be with them. Love them. Minister alongside of them. Show them how to follow Jesus by example. Serve rather than lead. As Dr John Guest put it, 'You have only two times when you must be faithful in preaching: in season and out of season.' Only two times! 'That's it.' Stay faithful. Fulfill God's purposes in the church and in the world through the ordinary means of grace.

We will have to teach our people this because the ways of the world have come into our churches. Many think they need a CEO. Others fancy that they would like an entertainer. Some wonder if they need a salesman. Yet what they really need is what the Great Physician ordered: *a pastor*. I am praying for you today as you prepare to obey your call and assume this role as the equipper of the saints.

Yours Faithfully,
Mike Milton.

9

INFANT BAPTISM

My dearest students in the pastoral ministry
and colleagues in the gospel of his grace,

There is no greater joy in the Christian ministry than holding an infant in your arms, slipping your hand into the baptismal font, scooping up water and pouring the covenantal waters over the child of Christian parents. If you are of the Baptist persuasion (and I am so thankful for your presence, my dearest in Christ) then you know the joy of which I speak – albeit in a service of dedication. You will please bear with me if I speak as a Presbyterian pastor in this little epistle, although I would desire that you apply this to your tradition.

The joy of infant baptism is so remarkable because, you, the pastor, are, personally, fulfilling the glorious Great Commission of our Lord and Savior Jesus Christ. In this there is unsurpassed vocational satisfaction. Now, I say that you are fulfilling the Great Commission because you are not only baptizing them but also inaugurating the child's journey of Christian nurture and growth as you and the family 'teach them whatsoever [Jesus Christ] taught'. The baptism is not only the beginning of the discipleship journey for the child, it is also a continuation of the covenant of God's grace which may extend back many generations, and may, by His mercy, extend to generations well beyond your life. Indeed, as it is in so much of our ministry, it is usual not to know the full fruit of the joy of your ministry of baptism (or, any part of your ministry) until you see in heaven that soul 'safe in the arms of Jesus' along with souls who were brought to Christ through successive generations.

Secondly, this is a great pastoral joy for you because it involves you, like no one else, in the private affairs of the family. This is the privilege of the pastor – to be where no one else is at the most critical stage of life. You're there at the beginning of life and you're there at the conclusion of life. I must say that I treasure this privilege above all others, save the preaching of the gospel of Jesus. My own love of the saints, and I dare say their love of their pastor, is shaped in those unforgettable moments of life. There's nothing like being with the family, hearing the stories of God's grace, and applying all the teaching, all the experiences, all the formal and informal internships you had under greater mentors, to the life of the family presenting their child to Jesus Christ.

Thirdly, you must always remember that baptism is a public event. We do not baptize in private. The sacraments of the Lord Jesus Christ are to be practiced by the Church, ordinarily, in public, and, ordinarily, by the ordained ministers of the church, because the baptism of an infant involves all of the congregation. They are all involved in that child's baptism, not only because of their vows to help rear the child in the church, but also because each baptism draws their hearts back to their own baptisms, or to the baptismal vows they took for their own children. As pastor, I seek to give the charge of the call to faithfulness not only to the baptismal family but also to the congregation.

There are practical ways that I have sought to use in order to remind the congregation of their involvement with the family and the child. When I am honored to baptize an infant, I normally seek to hold the child after baptism, and face the congregation as I give the charge to them. In this way they are able to see the little one. I remind them that this little one will grow up before them. This little child will come to understand the meaning of God's grace not only from his parents and from the Word of God and through the power of the Spirit of God, but also through them – through the people of God in the congregation he calls home.

As to the manner of baptism, according to our tradition, there are several features that I would want to stress. I would want to say, first, that there should be adequate preparation with the family as they approach the baptism. There should be a scheduled time spent with the family to discuss its meaning. I have found that this is most sweet when conducted in the home of the family. It is also a time to explain the gospel again (use every opportunity to recalibrate the family's faith back to the scarlet thread of redemption in God's covenant of grace in Jesus Christ). This involves private, pastoral conversation with the family. Beyond seeking to clarify and, hopefully, facilitate a deepening Biblical understanding of and appreciation for the sacrament of baptism, I also give father and mother (and brothers and sisters) something suitable to read and then to dialogue with each other and with me about what they have read.

I also remind the parents of several particulars about the service. I have been criticized for introducing such tactile functions into a graduate school of education, but I plead guilty to the charge. The seminary is a 'seedbed' of vocational preparation, not just scholarly research. We are instructing future pastors on mat-ters such as where one stands in a wedding or how one prepares for a graveside service, or, in this case, how to hold a child, and how to baptize, with Biblical fidelity and according to the best traditions of the Protestant church. For instance, I review each question, or vow, that will be taken in the presence of God and the witnesses in the worship service. I draw their attention to the charge to rear the child in the nurture and admonition of the Lord and what it means. I talk to them about family devotions. I meet with the father privately to speak the same words that I will charge publicly; namely, that he has the responsibility to be the veritable 'priest', if you will, in his own household. He is to conduct devotions within his home so that the children are indeed raised in the fear and the admonition of the Lord, and so that the teaching and preaching of the church are matched in the hearts and minds of children with their father's demonstrated faith. Many broken-hearted parents come to see that neglect of family devotions is an almost certain recipe for a crisis of faith in their child. Nothing is more important in the father's role in the home than opening the sacred Word and instructing his family. If there is no father in the home (as it was when I grew up as an orphan, and my Aunt Eva was the head of our home), then I would make a similar charge to a single mother, or other head of the household.

As to the baptism itself, as a part of a worship service, I remind the family that I expect the father to hold the child as the family comes to the baptismal font. It is a great tradi-tion, rich with (Scripturally derived) symbolism that should be practiced in our churches. There is plain precedent for it in the Word of the Lord. It was Zechariah who named John. The angel came to Joseph so that Joseph could name the Christ child, Jesus. So I instruct the father that as he and his wife bring the child to me, at the appropriate time in the service, and following the reading of Scripture and the explanation of the sacrament and the taking of vows, the father should place the child in my arms.

I cherish that blessed moment of the family placing their little one in the arms of one called to represent the church. It is a blessed privilege, dear pastor or pastoral student. I doubt that I shall ever know of a greater picture of pastoral ministry than the pastor holding a child of the church, surrounded by the family and the elders of the church, and the saints gathered in worship. What a picture! I remind the father that I will ask, 'What name is given this child?'

After hearing the name of the child, and while holding the child close to me, I then lean over the baptismal font (being careful that the congregation can see the event, for part of the means of grace expressed is through the vision of the baptism). As I hold the child over the baptismal font, I dip my hand into the font, and cup water with my right hand as I hold the child with my left hand, close to me, making sure that there is plenty of water seen (and heard dripping from my hand) by the congregation, and then pouring the (previously warmed!) water over the sweet head of the covenant child. While pouring the water, I repeat the blessed words of that glorious Trinitarian formula, 'I baptize you, _____, in the name of the Father, and of the Son, and of the Holy Spirit.'

At that sacred point in the service I turn toward the watching congregation and introduce them to the newest fellow member of the body – albeit a non-communing member (in the case of an infant or covenant child). I remind the saints that this child will grow up in their midst and that the impressions made upon this child, through the nursery, Sunday school, the children's ministry, the youth group, the college ministry, and all the ministries of the church, will shape the response, potentially, of thousands of human beings who might proceed from this child (through family generation or spiritual generation by that child's testimony). What we do in baptism has unimaginable positive consequences on human beings and even nations, through the successive generations, until the Lord Jesus Christ comes again.

I often have used a white linen napkin, which was embroidered by women of the church, to dry the head of the baby before placing the child in the arms of the mother. The napkin becomes a cherished token of remembrance of the service as well as a simple yet profound expression of support and Christian love from the congregation. I suspect that after all of these years of baptizing, there are many white linen napkins in family Bibles. As I return the child to the mother I speak to her, whispering to her, of her own unique holy obligation and joy outlined in the Word of God in not only loving her husband but also in shaping the consciences of her children. Each parent has his or her part to play in the rearing of the child. Thus, one of the most beautiful services in the church is accomplished.

It is my prayer that you who are being prepared by our pastor-scholars to become the next generation of godly gospel pastors will not only be faithful in preaching the inerrant and the infallible Word of the living God, but that also you will apply the blessed word of God in the sacraments. Of those two magnificent emblems of salvation, which Jesus Christ has left us, a continuity of the Old Testament ordinances of entrance into the church (circumcision) and redemption (Passover), I cannot say I treasure one over the other. I love both of them and have great pleasure in my soul thinking of the joy of administering these divinely given signs of salvation to the people of God as pastor. Yet, as I am focusing here on one of them, baptism, I do pray that God will bless you and that you will know the pastoral joy and vocational fulfillment that our Savior will most assuredly give to those who pastor His flock in His name as you welcome the children by baptism, 'for of such is the Kingdom of God.'

What a blessed joy it is for me to commend you, now, to Jesus Christ our Lord and to the Word of His grace and to the power of all of His promises, which are all 'yes and amen' through Him. Please know that I desire to be, now and always,

Yours Faithfully,
Mike Milton.

❧10❧

LAMBING SEASON

My Dear 'Pastor and Mrs _____, and Little Children',

Greetings and congratulations to you in the name of our Lord and Savior Jesus Christ! My friend, I remember, so vividly, you being in my study and speaking of the things of God and of the pastorate and of the stirring of the Lord in your life. I remember talking about how seminary would be a blessing to you. I saw your zeal and desire to grow deeper in the Word of God and the obvious call of Christ upon your life as a pastor. I knew that a good 'school of the prophets' such as Reformed Theological Seminary would be the place to help you prepare for a life of ministry. Now, to see those cherished moments of yesterday blessed of God today, and to see them come to fruition at this time, with your ordination and installation as a new pastor, must be a source of deep satisfaction to you and causes all of us to strengthen our trust in the God who truly completes what He starts (Phil. 1:7).

I pray blessings down upon your beloved wife and your dear children. I ask that the leadership of the church, and all the saints, will be happily united under their new pastor and in your biblical vision and mission for the kingdom of God, beginning in your community and unto the ends of the earth. My son in the faith, preach and pray, 'do the work of an evangelist,' counsel biblically, and serve your congregation out of the fullness of the Holy Spirit in your daily life of prayer. May you as the pastor of the congregation truly be an 'Enoch' who walks with God. Oh that your entire life and ministry would overflow from time spent with Jesus, and Jesus alone! Watch out for peddlers who would steer under-shepherds of Christ away from the ordinary means of grace in feeding His lambs. Word, sacrament, and prayer will call, convert, and sustain. Be a shepherd, not a CEO.

May your home life, my beloved sister in Christ, be a well-spring of warm and holy hospitality to those who need to know Jesus Christ through you! May your children come to love the church as they grow in the grace and admonition of the Lord with their father as their pastor! Help him to make your home a 'little church' for your family as much as you desire your church to be a 'little family' for others.

My own family sends their love and greetings to you all. I trust you will give my warm greetings to your new congregation and know that we are proud, in Christ, of you, excited about your ministry, optimistic about the work of Christ in you, and trust that I will always be,

Your very thankful old (former!) pastor, your servant and your colleague in the gospel of God's grace,

Mike Milton.

✣11✣

ONLY THE WORD

Our Dear Students,

'Modern pastoral theology is characterized largely by the study of what Anton T. Boisen, founder of the Clinical Pastoral Education movement in the Unites States, called "living human documents" – that is, the study of people, especially in their distress – rather than the study of biblical texts.'[1] This statement by Andrew Purves in his essential guide to Biblical pastoral theology, as demonstrated by such men as Martin Bucer and Richard Baxter, is one of the most important insights you will ever read. My beloved students in Christ, the work of the gospel minister in diagnosing and treating the human soul (and dare we allow other professions to hijack what God has called us to do) must find its beginning and ending in the inerrant and infallible Word of God. This is where you must go for the private ministry

---

1. Andrew Purves (2001), *Pastoral Theology in the Classical Tradition*, Westminster Press, 85.

of the Word, for your pastoral counseling. If you go elsewhere, then every area of your ministry will be infected by the rotting and untethered umbilical cord of the mind of man.

I mean to say that if your ministry focus is centered on the individual rather than on Christ's Word, your anthropology will be completely out of line. You must begin with what the Bible says about man and then move to ministry. In preaching, your ministry is about one man standing between 'two worlds' and announcing the gospel to broken man, to sinful man, and to man living with the consequences of original and actual sin. Your preaching addresses this, but you begin with the Word and move to people. This is the command of God to preachers: preach the Word to wounded man. It is not to preach the condition of wounded humanity and find some Word to uphold your observations.

Your evangelistic leadership of your congregation must also begin with the Word. Look out upon the world with a Biblical vision of compassion for the lost, but understand the vision by first seeing it in Scripture. To quote Purves again, 'Christ feeds His people, cares for them, brings in those who are lost, watches over them, and leads and provides for them so that they may grow in holiness.'[2] It is relying on the ordinary means of grace that transforms human beings in their various conditions, and it is the only method that brings vocational satisfaction. Don't cheat your future ministry by missing out on these years of studying Hebrew and Greek, Old Testament and New Testament, Systematic Theology and Church History. Don't miss out on studying Pastoral Theology that is grounded in God's Word. Beware of skipping to *Pastoring for Idiots* and all other sundry titles.

---

2. Purves, 85, 86.

This morning, as I was writing this letter to you, Bill stopped by to talk. He is a professional I have been counseling from my table at Starbucks. (I have always had public offices. Such a practice would be good for you as well. You need to find a way to meet people in the marketplace. You need to be where people live and where you can be accessible to them.) In the past several weeks Bill and I have been talking about a lot of things, particularly the downturn in the market. This has driven him to the brink of suicide. Literally. And the only thing I had to say to Bill, who has given up hope, was that if God was born in a feed trough, died on a cross, and was dead in a tomb, and yet lives, then there is hope. And Bill told me, 'That is the only thing I am counting on.' Well, Bill and my dear students, you can count on the Word to do what only the Word can do, and give you peace.

Yours Warmly in Christ,
Mike Milton.

❦12❦

EXPOSITORY PREACHING

Dear Students in the Pastoral Ministry,

How can we have an effective pastorate? How can our ministries, our preaching, support church health? How can we be faithful in our ministries?

There is a parable for young preachers in Walt Disney's *Dumbo*, the little circus elephant that had a hard time keeping up with mom and the other adults. He would latch his trunk onto the tail of the massive mammal in front of him and go with the herd! He was small, but with one critical attachment he could keep up.

How do we keep up as pastors in today's world? How do we even keep up with those who have gone before? How do we follow great preachers? How do we follow long pastorates? There are significant and divinely wise answers to those questions that may be located in the Bible, and cultivated through prayer, study, consecration, and dying to ourselves. But I want to consider one single answer today. I must try to answer it, without apology, from the Word of God. So, I ask you to join me, and turn to 2 Timothy 3:16 through to 4:1-5.[1] There, a little pastor named Timothy, just like the name of the mouse in *Dumbo*, who followed a ministry giant named Paul, is instructed on how to latch on to the legacy.

First, let the power and the possibility for failure sink in – Timothy was pastor of a church planted by Paul. When I feel really challenged, I think of Timothy. The elders at Ephesus had fallen on the neck of Paul and wept over his departure at Miletus (Acts 20:37-38). Three years of powerful ministry gave Paul the right to call them to shepherd the church of God that He had purchased with His own blood. And Paul, in his swan song at the twilight of his remarkable ministry, reminded Timothy regarding how he had to follow him. In doing so, he gave the secret to power. He lifted a mouse (no, his words were so divine and powerful that they transformed the mouse into an elephant), a giant became linked to his ministry, and linked to Jesus Christ, powered by Almighty God Himself. And what did Paul commend? He commended the Word of God, and after calling it God-breathed, he charged a God-called man to preach it. The answer to the question, 'How do mice latch on to elephants?' is neither original nor surprising at this conference. Like Charles Hodge addressing new

---

1. 'All Scripture is breathed out by God and profitable for teaching, for reproof, for correction, and for training in righteousness, that the man of God may be complete, equipped for every good work.

'I charge you in the presence of God and of Christ Jesus, who is to judge the living and the dead, and by his appearing and his kingdom: preach the word; be ready in season and out of season; reprove, rebuke, and exhort, with complete patience and teaching. For the time is coming when people will not endure sound teaching, but having itching ears they will accumulate for themselves teachers to suit their own passions, and will turn away from listening to the truth and wander off into myths. As for you, always be sober-minded, endure suffering, do the work of an evangelist, fulfill your ministry' (2 Tim. 3:16–4:5).

students at old Princeton, I, too, say to you, 'I glory in saying that you will learn nothing new here.' But it is an answer that every frail follower of pulpit giants must remember:

The only way for any of us to stand in the long and honorable legacy of gospel preachers is through expository preaching. Why? I offer eight concise reasons why expository preaching is the power for the pastorate, whatever your situation.

1. Expository Preaching is the Power of the Pastorate because it is Divinely Wrought. The way for Timothy to take his place as '[the] beloved child [of Paul]' (1.2), to latch onto the legacy of 'faith that dwelt first in [his] grandmother Lois and [his] mother Eunice' (1:5), to 'fan into flame the gift of God' (1:6) which was transferred through the apostolic laying on of hands of Paul himself (1:6), to overcome a 'spirit of fear' (1:7), to 'guard the good deposit entrusted to [him]' (1:14), to teach others what he has learned from Paul, thus extending the apostolic succession to another generation (2:1-2), to avoid getting 'entangled' with 'civilian pursuits' (2:4), to proclaim and teach the whole counsel of God, from the old covenant to the new covenant (as Paul speaks of in 2:8-13) 'for the sake of the elect that they may obtain the salvation that is in Christ Jesus with eternal glory', to take his place, to 'flee youthful passions and pursue righteousness' (2:22), and to do all of the things he is charged to do at Ephesus such as reminding the saints not to quarrel about words (2:14), to 'avoid irreverent babble' (2:16), to correct his opponents with the aim of leading them to repentance and a knowledge of the truth (2:25) so that they may avoid the 'snare of the devil' (2:26); to say it again, the way to conduct this ministry is by preaching the Word.

Paul makes it clear that the Word of God alone is able to meet the mission of the preacher. The reason this is so is that the Word of God is the authoritative instrument from the throne of

67

God to accomplish God's mission in the world. We remember that Paul's admonition to 'preach the word' follows his teaching that 'All Scripture is breathed out by God and profitable for teaching, for reproof, for correction, and for training in righteousness, that the man of God may be competent for every good work' (3.16-17).

I love the way Dr Robert L. Reymond put it: 'The Bible is a Word from another World.' In his *New Systematic Theology of the Christian Faith*, Reymond writes: 'When God gave his Word to us; he gave us much more than simply basic information about himself. He gave us the που στω, pou stō ("[a place] where I may stand"), or base that justifies both our knowledge claims and our claims to personal significance.'[2]

The Word of God is the place where the pastor may stand. Indeed, our very existence, our calling, our vocation only have meaning through this Word. I recently read J.C. Ryle's wonderful *Warning to the Churches*, in which the old Bishop of Liverpool warned his diocesan ministers of the perils they faced. The book left me amazed at his prophetic gifts and understanding of the times. I do not have such gifts, I am sure. But I do want to raise a danger related to the matter before us.

We live in an ever increasing iconoclastic culture that demands image and entertainment to communicate, that tells the preacher that short sound bites are more persuasive than exposition of a text, that narrative is of more importance than the exposition of a text, that postmodern man cannot endure direct teaching, but needs to make the homiletical turns for himself. I say that this is a danger to the preaching of the Word, to evangelism, and to discipleship. And in the midst of such an age, we would all do well

---

2. Robert L. Reymond (1997), *A New Systematic Theology of the Christian Faith*, Thomas Nelson, 111.

to remember that God called for Israel to do something that the heathen did not do, to think about him in His Word, and not in image. The God of the Jews was to exist in the Word and through the Word, an unprecedented conception requiring the highest order of abstract thinking. Iconography, thus, became blasphemy, so that a new kind of god could enter a culture. Those who are in the process of converting culture from word-centered to image-centered, might profit by reflecting on the Mosaic injunction.

The Word, my beloved brothers in the ministry, is the God-given place where we may stand, where we may reason, where we may dialogue with others. Indeed, we have been forbidden to go elsewhere. As a pastor, the reason that I want to focus on expository preaching – that is, proclaiming the inerrant and infallible Word of the living God as it is written, as it has been transmitted to me by God through the church, passing muster with the intent of the author, with conviction in my own life, and with love for those before me – is because expository preaching fixes itself, by its best definition, onto God's Word, divinely wrought and divinely authorized. This has powerful implications for my ministry that I want to explore further.

The only way for me to stand in the company of pulpit giants is to stand with this Word from another world. The truth is, if there are true giants in the church, if they are linked to Spurgeon, to Ryle, to M'Cheyne, to Whitefield, to Bunyan, to Luther, to Calvin, to Wycliffe, to Augustine, to Paul, to Jesus and the prophets, then they are men of this one Book, and that is all they have to say. This leads me to a second reason why we must cling to expository preaching in order to find our place in the accredited college of godly preachers.

2. Expository Preaching is the Power of the Pastorate because it is Biblically Faithful. We have seen that Paul tells Timothy to preach the Word, and we all know why. Preach the Word because the Word is divinely wrought. It is God's Word, and what could be nobler? If there were no other reason to proclaim His Word other than the mere fact that the Bible is His Word it would be enough. The matter, then, becomes how shall we do it? To 'preach' the Word must be to communicate it faithfully. Expository preaching, properly understood and properly done, fulfills this mandate.

Expository preaching is defined concisely and biblically by Albert Mohler in his contribution to *Give Praise to God: A Vision for Reforming Worship*: 'Expository preaching is that mode of Christian preaching that takes as its central purpose the presentation and application of the text of the Bible.'[3] And if expository preaching is really exposing the mind of God in a given text and communicating the mind of God to men and women, then no other methodology will do.

William Temple was not an expository preacher, though he said enough good things that I often quote him. But the former Archbishop of Canterbury did not believe that God would communicate His Word propositionally in the Bible because man could not understand it. He did believe, however, that we could understand what He wrote; otherwise, He wouldn't have written anything, but that is another argument! Enough to say, that if we believe that the power for our ministries is the Bible, as Paul teaches us, then it surely follows that expository preaching is the only model we should seek in communicating the Word.

As one who serves at a seminary and who is also a professor who gets to teach preaching every now and then, and who, as a pastor, gets to mentor younger preachers before sending them

---

3. R. Albert Mohler, 'Expository Preaching: Center of Christian Worship,' in *Give Praise to God* (2003), Presbyterian and Reformed, 112.

to other places of service, the subject of 'the future of expository preaching' in light of postmodernity and post-Christian America is a hot topic. I have found that many are wrestling with the question of whether such communication really can reach across the widening and ever-changing rivers of modern culture to grip the hearts and persuade the minds of an emerging generation. The realities of the emerging generation cause them to question expository preaching, and, in fact, have led several on a journey to 'find their voice', as they tell me, apart from the safe constraints of exposition. I'm happy to say that many with whom I have met have worked through that question to re-discover the power of expository preaching for this generation.

The whole matter of whether expository preaching can effectively communicate to a 'late modern' Western secularized culture is a question that has been posed and pondered by many. Yet if we are preaching the very Word of God, then surely God knows what we need in every age. This Word worked in the fallen ruins of Eden when God promised a Savior in Genesis 3:15. The Word worked in Genesis 12 when God's Word provided promises to Abraham for a land, a nation, and a blessing that would reach around the world. God's Word was enough in 586 BC in the crumbled remains of Jerusalem when a weeping prophet named Jeremiah preached with tears. God's Word worked in first-century Rome when Paul preached it. It worked in the eighteenth century in America when George Whitefield roared out its truths up and down the colonial coast. It worked in the nineteenth century in Korea when missionaries preached there, and it worked in industrial Dundee in Scotland when Robert Murray M'Cheyne preached there. It worked in the twentieth century, the bloodiest century so far in the world's history, when modernity overtook the West and men such as Martyn Lloyd-Jones thundered from a world capital such as London. And it will work in the twenty-first century, in postmodern and post-Christian North America, as it will work in China, Africa, India, and Europe. The Word will work in Chattanooga, will free slaves to sin in Miami, give abundant life in Los Angeles, renew cold-hearted saints in Des Moines, restore marriages in Peoria, reunite severed relationships in Louisville, sprinkle the spirit of holiness in New Orleans, call new missionaries out of Kansas City, and save souls from eternal punishment in Bangor, Seattle and Paducah. The power of our ministries is expository preaching because, if what we have to say is the Word of God, how we say it matters. And expository preaching, rightly followed, is the way to say it.

I have said that expository preaching is powerful because it is the Word of God and it is faithful to the Word of God. Let me continue with my reasons as to why it is the power for the pulpit, but let me be thoroughly pragmatic about it.

3. Expository Preaching is the Power of the Pastorate because it is Pastorally Effective. If this is the Word of God and it is, and if expository preaching is the biblically faithful method for giving out this Word of God, and it is, then it surely is the key to success in the pastorate.

What do I mean? I surely don't mean to imply that success and effectiveness in the pastorate are to be connected with being a celebrity, or selling books, or gaining fame. This past week I read a fine sermon by J.C. Philpot, from 1857, about the ever-present temptation of pride and vainglory among preachers, and I am aware that each of us deals in some way with this. But no, I'm not referring to that concern. Instead I'm talking about effectiveness in what I call the essentials of the ministry – gathering, growing and sending forth strong disciples of Christ. I have in mind the work of seeing souls saved, lives transformed, marriages saved, young people's hearts burning with zeal for Christ and His kingdom, and desiring to die to themselves in order to live for Christ. I have in mind 'setting in order the things that remain' and ordering our churches according to God's intentions. I have in mind speaking peace into a troubled, maybe even a splitting congregation. I have in mind being pastorally effective in shepherding the flock of God over whom He has made me an overseer. There is no program, no model, no paradigm, no experiment, no policy, and no amount of pure elbow grease or mental genius that can equal the power of the Word of God preached. It accomplishes everything I hope for in the ministry. Recently, I read that the best time-tested discipleship tool in the history of the church has been morning and evening worship in which there is expository preaching. My own experience as a disciple and a pastor is that I couldn't agree more.

When I counsel people in trouble, I always ask if they are sitting under the expository preaching of the Word of God. I'm not asking them to come to my church, though I would love to have them. I'm simply saying that they must locate a place to belong, a local congregation, where the preacher is committed to moving sequentially through the Word of God – that may be moving through books, chapters, or other preaching portions within a book – in such a way that they are getting the mind of Christ in the study. Expository preaching is pastorally effective.

4. Expository Preaching is the Power of the Pastorate because it is Vocationally Satisfying. When I say 'vocationally satisfying', I am speaking to those who have come, in their own lives, to say with Paul in 1 Corinthians 9.16: 'For if I preach the gospel, that gives me no ground for boasting. For necessity is laid upon me. Woe to me if I do not preach the gospel!' If we are called by God to preach the Word of God to a dying world, and if preaching is unveiling the mind of God for man in this Word, and this is what expository preaching is, then it follows that we will only be happy in our work if we are doing so!

Eugene Peterson is the pastor's friend in so many ways. I have greatly benefited from his various works. In *Under the Unpredictable Plant*, he tells how he was at the point of burnout at Christ the King Presbyterian Church in Belaire, Maryland. He was going from board meeting to board meeting, doing this and that, and as a pastor who has planted two churches (and Peterson's church was a church plant) I know how it can be. The tired pastor goes to his session and tells them that he can't go on. He thinks he is at the end of his pastorate. Fatigue is physical exhaustion, and we all get that. Burnout is a loss of meaning, and we do not necessarily have to have that, but this is apparently what Peterson had. His session was wise and told him to list the things he went into the ministry to do. He listed preaching, visiting the sick, sharing the gospel, and the other matters that the Bible teaches us is our work. His session told him, 'You do those things you were called to do, and we will do the rest.' You probably have read what happened. He not only was renewed in his ministry, but also stayed over thirty years at that church.

If God has called you to preach, he has not called you to be a conference chairman, a religious store manager, or even a great storyteller. There are many who will tell us that expository preaching is not enough. Peterson says, 'Propagandists are abroad in the land lying to us about what congregations are and can be. They are lying for money. They want to make us discontent with what we are doing so we will buy a solution from them that they promise will restore virility to our impotent congregations. The profit-taking among those who market these [programs] indicates [that] pastoral gullibility in these matters is endless.'[4]

---

4. Eugene Peterson (1994), *Under the Unpredictable Plant: An Exploration*

Let us not be gullible. Expository preaching fulfills God's purpose for our lives as preachers. He has called you to preach the Word, and you will never be happy until you go to that Word, live in that Word, exegete the meaning of that Word, dive like a Pacific native to the bottom of the ocean for the rich pearls of that Word, and then come back up from your time in the deep-blue of God's presence, string those pearls together in a sermon, and put them on the neck of your people.

Only a preaching method, a preaching approach, that is radically Word-centered, Christ-centered, Gospel-saturated, and uncompromisingly faithful to the text will give you joy. For you were made to preach.

5. Expository Preaching is the Power of the Pastorate because it is Eschatologically Useful. When I say eschatologically useful, I am saying that expository preaching brings our people into contact with ultimate realities. In personal eschatology, expository preaching prepares our people to not only live but to die. Oh, if we could hear the stories of faithful preachers, seated right here today, who have shared those sweet and sacred moments of vigil with a family when a loved one is going home to heaven. You know that the power for your ministry at that time is in the exposition of the Word. An elder in our church who recently went to be with the Lord said, 'I have been waiting for this. I am ready to go home.' This attitude comes from expository preaching.

Expository preaching also is eschatologically useful in that it brings our people to see God's ultimate cosmic realities. I would say that faithful exposition of the Word would probably distance our preaching from some of the excessive, isogetical proposi-

---

in Vocational Holiness, Eerdmans, 18.

tions that we sometimes hear at certain prophecy seminars that lead to theological speculation and seem to draw cosmic curiosity seekers. But faithful exposition, say of 1 Corinthians 15 or Ephesians 1, leads our people to see that God is a teleological God, that this world is going somewhere, and that we who are God's children are destined for something greater than ourselves.

The revelation of God gives meaning, purpose, and context to time, space, and eternity, to man and God. It gives meaning to sickness, hope, and even happiness in the face of theodicy, and the questions of suffering.

6. Expository Preaching is the Power of the Pastorate because it is Personally Edifying. The call to preach the Word is a blessing. Each week we come to the text, and we are fed by it, hopefully, before we give it to others. I know the James 3 warning against being teachers, but we also know the words of Paul that this Word will 'make you wise for salvation' (2 Tim. 3:15). We will save ourselves as well as those who hear us.

I must say this, also. When we are about the work of expository preaching in the pastorate, the work carries us along in a sense. Week-in and week-out, we develop a discipline of study, for to preach the Word of God line-upon-line, precept-upon-precept, demands time, struggle, and prayer. I know that in this room, your heads and hearts are turning, perhaps not over this address, but over the portion of Scripture that you must deliver this week. Is there anything as rewarding in life as unburdening your soul in that movement when you approach the sacred desk and open up the Bible? Expository preaching feeds my soul. I know of no other way to put it.

7. Expository Preaching is the Power of the Pastorate because it is Constantly Challenging. To present the mind of Christ in a text requires much of us, does it not? I once heard a preacher say that every time he preached, a little piece of him died. I am sure there are those for whom that is true because they are tired of preaching, or they will know that they will get ripped to pieces at the front door of the church. But this man was speaking about preaching in a way that I can identify with. Like you, to preach the mind of God, to go through the necessary steps to get there, then to emotionally discharge the holy calling on your life through the act of expositing a text, is the most challenging thing in the world. It takes your very life.

I was once in a seminar with the late Dr D. James Kennedy where seminary students were allowed to ask him anything they wanted. One asked, 'Dr Kennedy, what is the most challenging thing you have ever done in the ministry?' His answer was, 'Prepare next Sunday's sermon.' We all know it is true. We all know that such rigorous preaching cut short the life of John Calvin. It must be balanced with recreation and separation unto God in quiet prayer and reflection. We all know that to face constantly the Word of God each and every week, sometimes three or four times each week, is overwhelming at times. But for those called to do so, it is a response to an amazing love that demands my soul, my life, my all. Would you really want it any other way?

8. Expository Preaching is the Power of the Pastorate because it is Always Contemporary. When we preach the Word, we never have to worry about whether it is the right time or not, or if it is the right message or not. Now surely wisdom is needed to discern between preaching Lamentations at a wedding or Leviticus 15 and 'bodily discharges' at the baptism of an infant! But, you know what I mean. As I think about this conference, I am reminded once more that expository preaching is always in vogue, always 'cool', if you will, for the human condition remains the same in every age.

Conclusion

How did Martyn Lloyd-Jones follow G. Campbell Morgan? Expository preaching. How did James Boice follow Donald Grey Barnhouse? Expository preaching. How did Timothy follow Paul? 'Preach the Word.' We must guard what was deposited to us with expository preaching. We must, because we can't conduct a sound ministry of visitation of the sick and dying without it. We cannot carry on the work of evangelism, discipleship, world missions, building up the saints, or being a witness to our communities without expositing the Word from another world. We were made for it. It is our lives. It is our heart.

Readers of great missionary stories will recall the amazing life of the intrepid Scot, the physician David Livingstone, who, like Lloyd-Jones, was not only a medical doctor but also a preacher of the gospel. After he died, Livingstone's body was returned from Africa in order to be buried with highest honors in Westminster Abbey in London. Before his body was taken from the deepest parts of that great continent on a seven hundred mile trip to the coast, the natives of the place where he died so loved him that they removed his heart and buried it in the place where he had preached the gospel. Jesus said in Matthew 6:21: 'For where your treasure is, there your heart will be also' (NIV). The tribesmen knew that David Livingstone's treasure was Africa. His soul would go to his Savior, his body would return, for the time being, to his native country, but Livingstone's heart remained in Africa. Do our people know that we treasure them? Do they know that we treasure preaching the gospel of God to them? Do they know where our hearts are?

I was the twelfth pastor of a church that was started in 1838. The men who went before me were greatly loved. I followed one of the greatest Christian communicators of the twentieth century. Dr Ben Haden remains a close friend. He followed a man whose name is engraved on everything from the YMCA to a homeless mission. He followed a beloved pastor who died five years into office but whose five years left an impression of ministry that was felt for six decades after his death. He followed a former Confederate chaplain who led a veritable civil rights campaign for African-Americans in the late 1800s in that community. He served for fifty years. He always wore a clerical collar and always left on the light of the porch of the manse 'just in case someone needs a minister'.

I once asked some of the older folks in the congregation about my predecessors. 'Why are they still venerated so? What was it about them that made them so special?' I heard various answers from different people, but always a common denominator. The reason why my predecessors are so honored is that they preached the Word to a certain people in a certain time in a certain place. That Word did for those people in their land, in their time, what the Word always does – it saves, changes lives, heals, restores, gives hope, brings assurance, and brings God to men and men to God. I am convinced that in the final analysis, this is the answer. All preachers, whether they consider themselves mice or elephants, great or small, are loved when they faithfully open up the Bread of Life and feed the lambs of Jesus. And this becomes our legacy, not that our images are recorded in oils to hang on a church wall, but that our hearts are buried in the place where we took our stand, spent our years, and gave our lives to preach the Word. For, you see, to those whose lives are changed, you will always be a giant to them. Amen.

Yours Faithfully,
Michael A. Milton, Ph.D.

❧13❧

ON THE PREPARATION OF THE PASTORAL PRAYER

My Dear Students,

I know that one of your primary concerns as you consider your calling to the pastorate is sermon preparation. And this is right. Yet you must not relegate the preparation of the pastoral prayer to a lesser place.

Dr James Fowle, one of my predecessors at the historic First Presbyterian Church of Chattanooga, was 'accused' of spending more time on the pastoral writing and Biblical research of the 'long prayer' than he did on his sermon! But the older folks who told me that information also told it to me with a smile and a fondness for him as their pastor. He loved them. He must have known and believed what I have also found to be true, that the preparation of the pastoral prayer is in some ways the culmination of your weekly pastoral work.

The rhythms of ministry bring you in and out of the joys of weddings and births, the good news of business successes, and the joyful sight of new friendships springing up. These are things that would make any father smile (and you will be a pastoral 'father' of the Father's flock). Yet you will also walk the cancer wards, and sit beside families going through death vigils. In the same week that you counsel a happy young couple with their bright future ahead of them you will also be present at that most dismal and horrid place of our generation: the family court. Here is where the past years of marriage are undone. Property and children and rights are divided up, with one lawyer on one side of the court lobby and another lawyer on the other side, and you are in-between them with tears and pleas for reconciliation. You will bring the comforts of Christ to that which will not be mended on earth.

You will be there for a child's first birthday party of the family for whom you prayed through their adoption process, and you will be there with another couple mourning yet another miscarriage. All of these things come to the one who has heard deep in his soul, 'Feed my lambs. Tend my lambs. Feed my sheep. Follow me' (John 21:15, 16, 17, and 19). And so you must. But remember, my beloved in Christ, you go with the means that Christ has appointed unto you: word, sacrament and prayer.

It is about prayer that I want to speak to you now. You must, as a core and essential Biblical job description of being a pastor of the Lord's chosen people, give yourself to prayer as well as to the ministry of the Word (Acts 6:4). Through these 'ordinary' (yet quite extraordinary) means given by the Lord Himself, you will discharge the duties of your office and you will also see the blessings of God. The growth of the congregation in the grace and knowledge of God, as well as in its fulfilling the purposes of God in the world, are all linked organically, scripturally and supernaturally to those means.

81

Thus, your pastoral prayer in the worship service is of primary use for the blessing of the people of God as you come to the Lord on their behalf. We think immediately of the best models of this in the Word of God with Moses interceding for the children of Israel, with Jesus Himself in John 17, or with Paul's tender reminders in his letters of his prayers for his readers. So considering that you would agree that this prayer, the 'long prayer' as our fathers often called it, or the 'pastoral prayer' as we are more likely to call it, ought to be shaped by the following rubrics:

1. The pastoral prayer should come out of the pastor's heart for the people and his calling as a pastor. No pastor can truly pray with unction of the Spirit who is not called to pastor, nor called to pastor a certain people, nor has tasted of the divine fire of the altar of God in his own devotional life. Therefore, the pastoral prayer emerges out of the pastor's devotional life that is spiritually connected to the people of God.

Such a pastor has been at the bedside and has interceded there first before ascending to the pulpit to pray on the Lord's Day. As a pastor you stand with your face to the Lord and your back to the people at one place in the pastoral prayer, and yet you turn to face the people with God's promises and assurances in another place in the prayer. You are the pastor who has wept in the secret of your car on the way home from a visit with a man who has refused God. You are broken by the sin of mankind in general and your people in particular, broken by the suffering of mankind in general and your people in particular, and broken in your own heart and life over your inability to grasp the incomprehensibility of the Lord, the mysteries of God in salvation, in healing, in saving, and in His timing of all of these things. You may thus turn to the Lord in your prayer, and cry out with the heart of Jesus beating in you, 'My God, my God!' The people know that their pastor is *with* them in the fields and is thus *for* them in the pulpit.

2. The pastoral prayer should come out of meditation on the Word of God. I ordinarily would never enter the pulpit to pray unless the prayer in my heart is symbiotically connected to a passage in the Bible. I may or may not carry notes on the prayer into the pulpit, although my files are replete with pastoral prayers written over the years. As I am preparing even now to offer a pastoral prayer at a church, I am studying John 17. I am concerned that when Jesus says that He is praying not only for Himself (the first part of the high priestly prayer), and for the disciples (the second part), but also for those who will believe through their testimony. My focus is on how to pray this to the Lord in such a way that blessing is also rained down upon the quenched souls of those who feel alone and distant from God, or feel as if no one could reach their prodigal children. I am praying, as it were, with my back to the Lord and my face to the people, and my prayer is structured upon Jesus' prayer in that blessed passage. Yet, I turn to the Lord and remember that the unity that Jesus prayed for, through the witness of His disciples, needs to be in the life of the congregation. This unity needs to be visible between husbands and wives, and children and parents, in the relationship of the elders and the pastors, and in the deacons and the elders. It needs to be in the heart and mind of the one who feels alone and abandoned by God and man, perhaps the widow in the nursing home, but also in the twelve-year-old girl who, that morning, may feel betrayed by another girl seated two rows behind her.

In other words, having exegeted the passage, I now offer expository, intercessory pastoral prayer to the Lord in the power of the Spirit who breathed out the Scripture. I am concerned as I move through these intercessions, that the Lord who prayed that through the unity of the people, in unity with the apostles and prophets and martyrs and saints who have gone before and who worship across the face of the earth, the world would believe that the Father had sent the Son (John 17.21); that the world would know of the glory of the Son in the glory of the church, that others not yet in the congregation would come to be saved and placed by God in the assembly of the faithful.

Thus, my meditation upon this text has led me in my inter-cessions from considering Christ and His disciples, to those who sit before me, to considering a plea for unity in the families and individual lives of people who need to be reconciled to each other. But now I am disturbed in my spirit, and thus praying out of that divine discontentment, that more would come to know Christ, that more would come to share in the glory of being a son or daughter of God! My prayers, started in scriptural meditation, have climbed the stairs of biblical truth to seek divine remedy for the people with a crescendo of 'Oh God, save your people!'

I have prepared notes, written out full manuscripts, and prayed not only without any rubrics to help me, but prayed out of my soul moved just by looking upon the flock before me. I have sometimes prepared a prayer and then let my eyes move across the congregation before the services began or perhaps during a hymn, and the Holy Spirit has convicted me that I must pray in a different fashion, from a different passage of Scripture, or with a different focus. This is of the Lord and I am not seek-ing to be mysterious or super-spiritual, but acknowledging that if you are saturated with the Word of God and with prayer in your life for your people, coming from having actually been with them, then such phenomena will happen. And I know this will happen to you.

Don't be concerned about the prayer that you prepared, but the prayer that the Spirit prepared in you to pray for His people.

Remember we shepherd His people. We feed them on Word and sacrament and prayer. But among the ways that we pray, none is more precious to the people than when their pastor prays for them, out of love, out of personal experience of their trials and joys, and out of the abundance of the pastor's time with God and His Word. In this way, then, the pastoral prayer cultivates the hearts of the people to receive the balm of heaven in the sermon, and opens up the heart of the pastor to receive the Spirit of God in His Word.

I could not preach if I had not prayed. More specifically, I could not have preached God's Word to them unless I had prayed God's Word for them. I am thinking of you, students in the study of the pastoral ministry whether it be on the mission field or in the local church or as an evangelist planting a church, and I am, on this Lord's Day, praying for you.

Yours Faithfully,
Michael A. Milton.

❧14❧

MINISTERING PASTORALLY

Dear Students of the gospel of Christ,

There is something that is on my heart; something that I need to unburden myself of, and it is this: you minister to people best when you minister out of Christ's compassion for the broken people God has placed in your life. Because all truth is God's truth, this applies in other contexts, but its incarnational glory is fully displayed in the life and ministry of Christ our Lord. As a believer and a preacher of the gospel I minister out of the center point of my life and my vocation – my faith in Jesus Christ.

In the ninth chapter of Matthew's Gospel, our Lord and Savior Jesus Christ is revealed as the great God of profound compassion. As one reads through the chapter that leads to the climactic moment when His great heart is fully revealed as a broken heart for the multitudes, Matthew shows how Jesus had ministered. In the Lord's compassion, He had healed the sick, forgiven reprobates, and raised the dead. He moved through the layers of hurting humanity with healing in His hands.

Jesus Christ ministered to everyone who needed ministry. He went throughout all the villages feeling every disease. There was inevitability about it all. 'He will go on healing everyone,' it seems. Thus it was recorded in Matthew 4:23-24: 'And he went throughout all Galilee, teaching in their synagogues and proclaiming the gospel of the kingdom and healing every disease and every affliction among the people. So his fame spread throughout all Syria, and they brought him all the sick, those afflicted with various diseases and pains, those oppressed by demons, epileptics, and paralytics, and he healed them.' So in 9:35: 'And Jesus went throughout all the cities and villages, teaching in their synagogues and proclaiming the gospel of the kingdom and healing every disease and every affliction.'

Yet the Son of Man came to a point in Matthew's account that He looked on the multitude as sheep without a shepherd; scattered (not a 'dispersed' kind of scattering but the Greek means a 'downcast' and 'ravaged' form of scattering). It was then that Matthew – a sinful tax collector converted by the compassion of Jesus Christ and who, in this ninth chapter, placed himself in his own writing like a Rembrandt in his own painting – reveals the love of our Savior. Matthew tells us that Jesus had *compassion* on the multitude for they were like sheep without a shepherd. The Greek expression for compassion is a word that speaks of the very intestines of our Savior – the deep inner organs that were wracked with pain – the pain of a compassion that no one can ever comprehend. It is the compassion of the Creator for His own creation. It is the compassion of a father for his children but in an infinitely more intimate relationship of love than you or I could ever fathom.

Out of this deep-seated compassion of our Lord Jesus comes His command that His disciples should pray. And for what or whom should they pray? 'Then He said to His disciples, "The harvest is plentiful, but the laborers are few; therefore pray earnestly to the Lord of the harvest to send out laborers into his harvest'" (Matt. 9:37-38).

Christ therefore looks confidently over the landscape of a broken, fallen humanity and sees redemption on its way. Yet the redemption will come to the multitudes through His disciples. And those disciples will develop out of prayer for laborers for His harvest. You have heard of preachers who were called by God to preach who later learned of, say, a great-grandfather who prayed each day that God would bless his progeny with a minister of the gospel. That example, a very common one, is a direct response to this passage.

But here's the thing that I want to say: the multitudes that Jesus saw were the objects of His divine affection; the objects of His compassion; the aim of His redeeming purposes. And yet, Jesus, according to John 17, would love those who were not yet even born. And He would do so through the testimony of His disciples. So Jesus Christ had compassion on the multitude that day. Matthew tells us this. But John lets us know that the compassion of Jesus extends beyond those people to generations yet unborn and to disciples yet unconverted.

Jesus Christ's compassion would be extended to others through the very disciples who received His compassion themselves. Therefore, Jesus' prayer for shepherd-laborers to go into the plentiful harvest is a prayer for you and me. It is a prayer that we should reach the multitudes in our day, people He made, souls He has elected unto salvation. Yet we can only reach those who are before us. We aim our message at one, or two, or three, the people we know who need the Lord. Yet if I reach out to those who are on my heart, and you reach out to those who are on yours, and others reach out to the people that are on theirs, then we shall reach many together. This is the plan of Jesus. This is our calling.

In short: minister to the people God has placed on your heart. There are probably only a few, but because all of us are in the same condition, if you minister to that person on your heart, you will minister to many others who are in the same condition.

I give an example from my life. I have a broken heart about two people I once knew. One of them I wish that I could have known better. But that is part of the necessary beckoning, the acute aching, the deep passion, and the God-given desire to reach them and bridge the distance, and bring the redemptive relief of healing to their souls through Jesus.

Who are the people from the multitude that God has placed in your life? Name them. Those are the precious souls for whom Christ has compassion. Minister to those few in your heart and you'll actually minister to many. Minister Christ personally and you will minister him pastorally. And Christ's command will become an answered prayer.

Faithfully Yours,
Mike Milton.

❦ 15 ❦

LEADERSHIP THROUGH CHANGE

My Dearest Students of RTS Charlotte,

As you leave your seminary community some of you will be called to be assistant pastors. Others will be called to be solo pastors. Some of you will become church planters or missionaries. But however the Lord leads you, one thing is for sure: you will be involved, personally, with the matter of change.

Change is a word that strikes fear in the heart of every parishioner! And truth be told, the same is true of all of us. But change is part of the ministry. Continuity and discontinuity, hidden and revealed, old and new: these Biblical concepts are reflected in our lives and in our churches. Indeed, your very presence one Sunday morning as a new minister in a local church community means that there will be change in that congregation.

Nothing is more difficult to navigate than change. But through patience, waiting on the Lord, and remembering that God was at work before you arrived will help you in the journey and to come out on the other side still in the ministry.

I recently came across an article by Michael Duduit, the editor of *Preaching.com*, who interviewed Stuart Briscoe, the noted pastor, author, and speaker. I offer an excerpt that might be helpful on this topic: 'Briscoe's call to the pastorate ushered him into a role for which he had no experience and little training. He experienced some bumps and bruises learning pastoral ministry the hard way; but he did learn, and today Elmbrook Church (where he continues to serve as Minister-at-Large, after 30 years as Senior Pastor) continues to benefit from the wonderful leadership he provided for three decades.'

Among the leadership insights he notes:

* Don't be hasty in introducing change.

* Don't knock down a fence until you know why it was put up in the first place.

* Do present solid biblical and commonsense reasons for change.

* Do present change as a proposal, not a fait accompli.

* Do allow time for reaction, and don't fail to listen to objections.

* Do invite suggestions, and don't hesitate to incorporate the best ones.

* Do give people a chance to take ownership of the change.

* Don't be disappointed by naysayers, and don't forget you're still their pastor.

'Leading people through change is one of the major tasks of the pastor. Briscoe's counsel can help us all to learn to do so with wisdom and grace.'

I couldn't agree more. I want to write to you again on some thoughts that I usually give to pastors who ask me, 'How should

I enter this new work?' But for now think about the list of Stuart Briscoe's insights. And if you ever want to talk about it, just call and set up a time for us to talk. That is why I am here.

Yours warmly in the gospel,
Mike Milton.

16

ADVICE FOR A SEMINARIAN

Dear Students in the Gospel of Christ,

Recently, I was asked by a young wife and mother to write some thoughts on ministry reflections for her husband, a seminarian. I thought you might benefit from my reply.

'Here are some reflections on your insightful question: As I look back on the season of life that your husband is in, I would…

+ Thank God even more for a faithful wife who was made by God to help me with wisdom and insight into the challenges I face and the opportunities I have. I would listen more carefully to her God-given intuitive understanding of how I could be a better father, husband and man of God.

+ Listen more and enjoy the changing cycles of growth in John Michael, our son. Enjoy the present stages in your little ones' lives; soon they will pass. I often asked my son, all through his growing up, 'Son, do you know what my favorite age is for a boy?' He soon learned that I would say his age back to him. Recently I asked him that and he told me, 'Dad, I think it is (pause…) seventeen!!!' 'Yes, son, that is my favorite age for a child.' Yet don't just say it. Take time to soak up the unique blessings and challenges of every age of your children.

+ Discipline more with honey and not only with the rod. I would seek to help them understand that obedience really is better and leads to greater blessings, more 'treats', if you will.

+ Build more margins into my life, remembering life and ministry is a marathon, not a sprint.

+ Follow the example of Edwards, Washington[1] and others, earlier than I did, to study the wisdom of others and write a personal resolution or covenant with the Lord.

+ Pray more.

+ Smile more.

+ Be less concerned about spilled milk and more concerned about wasted time.

+ Play more board games with my family.

+ Watch even more old classic movies with my family during the sweet holiday seasons. I recommend doing so in flannel pajamas, holding all of your children in your lap until they fall asleep. Big bowls of ice cream are highly recommended at such times. Then I would spend time with my wife and good hot chocolate, and more classic movies (but this time holding her in my lap)!

1. See the prayer journal of George Washington in William Jackson Johnstone (1919), *George Washington, the Christian*, The Abington Press, 24-35.

- Sing more old hymns at night before bed.

- Spend more time in yard work, feeling the good earth in my hands, and helping my family to see the joy of tending a garden together. Gardening teaches so much. It is a tonic for the soul. Children will always remember the time of learning lessons from dad in the garden.

And some practical advice for your husband:

- Read *A Cotter's Saturday Night* by Robert Burns and keep the family devotional light on each night. Don't let your family leave for school and you for your daily work until you have read the Word and offered morning prayers.

- Pray over and bless your wife and children by name. The voice of a father speaking a child's name before the Lord in prayer will make an indelible mark on the soul of a child. It will also bind the heart of the wife to her husband in an even greater way. This is a satisfying and fulfilling way to care for your family spiritually, not just materially. In fact, the spiritual role gives meaning to the other roles as provider of the family.

- Recognize that, in work, as in ministry, you cannot serve out of an empty reservoir. Spend more time in prayer. Read widely and deeply. Keep sermon outlines simple. Less is more. Slower is more effective.

- Anticipate your appointments. Be fully present with others. Then reflect on what God is saying to you through that appointment or ministry event or person.

- Consider difficulty as part of the minister's job description. Be caring but don't enter the infected wounds of others. Be a good physician of the soul. Look beyond presenting issues to find real issues. Never respond to criticism without taking it to the Lord first and asking, 'Lord, what is important and what should I not be concerned with?' Worry less and talk more with the Lord.

- Love God. Love people. Love prayer and the Word and let the sacraments recalibrate you as a minister and a believer back to the cross.

- Never do ministry alone. Always invest in others and always multiply ministry.

- In all areas of life, begin each day with a prayer: 'Lord, keep me broken at the foot of the cross.'

So those are my humble thoughts. I pray that you can use some of this advice from one broken person to another. God bless and keep you. You and your families are the treasures we exist to reach and send forth into the harvest fields of the Lord.

Yours Faithfully,
Mike Milton.

❦17❦

ON LEANING TOWARDS WORKS IN OUR MINISTRY

Dearest Student in Christ Jesus and the Vocation of the Pastorate,

My heart is greatly filled with prayer for you this morning over one thing: when you become a director of the consciences of the people whom you will serve, you must make sure that your own conscience is right with God. I am chiefly concerned that all will be right with God over this one thing: that you believe that no supernatural goals can be achieved without the supernatural work of the Lord God.

Thomas Boston recorded in his notes on Mr Fisher's *Marrow of Modern Divinity*: 'I dread mightily that a rational sort of religion is coming in among us; I mean by it, a religion that consists in a bare attendance on outward duties and ordinances, without the power of godliness: and thence people shall fall into a way of serving God, which is a mere deism, having no relation to Jesus Christ and the Spirit of God.'[1]

---

1. Edward Fisher, *The Marrow of Modern Divinity*, ed. William VanDoodewaard (2009, Christian Focus Publications), 37.

There is nothing new under the sun and the devil is insidiously repetitive in his diabolical methods to minimise the gospel of God in our ministers' hearts and thus in our people by tricking them into thinking that 'doing things' will promote the ends of Christ. There is nothing I fear more in today's world than ministers of Christ who steer their people toward a religion (and I have seen this in conservative congregations and in self-styled progressive congregations) that seeks to 'serve' God by activities.[2]

'In all views which fallen man has towards the means of his own recovery, the natural bent is to the way of the covenant of works.'[3] Thus while I applaud a liturgical renewal, and a return to thoughtful, Biblical and orderly worship orders, we must remember what Martyn Lloyd-Jones observed – that when there is a rise in liturgy there is a simultaneous decline in expository preaching. Why not have both? It will take a minister of the gospel who sees both worship and preaching as part of the same supernatural means, and so both will be bathed in much prayer.

Indeed, the minister who leads the service after spending time with Almighty God in the secret places will be a minister that people will follow – follow, that is, to Christ and to have humble, reverent hearts before Him. Here at our seminary you will receive training in the classical expository method, in which we believe wholeheartedly. Yet, should you begin to compose your sermons without prayer or with confidence in a system of homiletical style, then Satan will have fooled you or you will have fooled yourself.

God honors His Word, and God wants ministers whose hearts have been cut by that Word in their own devotions. Only

---

2. Additionally, this sort of innate, natural bent towards achieving goals through human means will show up in counseling and in leading (which should really be 'serving' because there is no other way to 'lead' than to serve).

3. Fisher, 35.

when you can preach the message for that week to yourself, and come under the conviction of it, will you be ready to give it to others. The messenger, in this case, must open up the seals and read the sacred words from heaven and Ezekiel-like eat them, digest them, and know their convicting powers in his own life. When you say, 'Open your Bibles to John chapter one,' or some other passage, will you be ready to preach?

We must be vigilant in these matters. Souls are at stake. An entire generation waits, like red winter wheat kernels under the frozen ground of such religion, for the minister of the gospel to thaw the field of ice with the heat of a personal and devout love of Jesus Christ in his own heart and a preaching that flames forth with the fire of a tongue that has touched the holy altar of heaven.

To maintain this attitude I offer nothing but the old paths that have served every generation, every ethnic group, every part of Christ's kingdom and every man of God. I encourage you to pray. Pray with methods that include adoration, confession, thanksgiving and supplication. Pray daily as a part of your work as a minister. Let other things go, but pray first. Then go to parish work. Pray first, pray daily, pray through the Scripture like M'Cheyne. Pray through the church year, pray for souls that are close to you, pray for other ministers and missionaries and gospel workers, for authorities in the church and in the state and in your own life. Pray for the weak (keeping a list of those in need and frequently inquiring as to how the Lord is answering prayer). And pray for yourself. Pray that God will infuse you with power from on high to conduct your sacred calling.

I encourage you to look for new seasons of life and ministry when you turn again to Christ and plead for the Holy Spirit to come upon you and anoint you for ministry. We must not dismiss the fact that we need the power of God to come down and touch us, move us, and make our theology burn with the brightness of the risen Christ in it. The moment you get sucked into a system of thought that says that you can grow your church through man-made methods, or grow believers through programs that do not incorporate or, better yet, lean hard on the Word of God and the Spirit of God in prayer, then you are in grave danger as a minister. Your people are in danger. So think on these things.

The spirit of the age is drawing us, yet again, in the church to believe that we must do other things, be more culturally relevant, more in touch with what unbelievers want, more theologically sophisticated, more intellectual, and more this and more that. But the Word of God calls us to simply follow close to Jesus in Word, sacrament and personal and public prayer. Then when we have touched heaven with our souls through these means of grace, and only then, can we turn to our people on the Lord's Day and say, 'I call you to the public worship of the living God.'

I close with Luther's charge in this area to his students: 'I warn each of you, and especially such as are to be directors of conscience, that you exercise yourselves in study, reading, meditation, and prayer, so as you may be able to instruct and comfort both your own and other's consciences in the time of temptation, and to bring them back from the law to grace, from the active [or working] righteousness; in a word, from Moses to Christ.'[4]

Thus, in my own prayers, I am praying for you in these things.

Yours Faithfully,
Mike Milton.

4. Martin Luther, *Commentary on Galatians*, as quoted by Thomas Boston in his notes on *The Marrow*, 37.

❧18❧

PREACH ONE SERMON

Dear Pastoral Students in the Gospel of Christ,

I want to bring you a charge as we approach the conclusion of this semester of study. My charge to you is to preach one sermon. You read that correctly: one sermon. What do I mean?

If we read Paul correctly, then the former blasphemer could never get over the grace of God that forgave and called 'an insolent man' into the ministry of His Son, Jesus Christ. It is not hyperbole to say, as we survey the life of Paul, that he really only had one sermon. Of course, the great man of God would preach the gospel in different contexts, using various messages, and explaining new covenant theology in Christ Jesus out of the Old Testament to diverse people. He was, most certainly, as we remind you to be, 'true to the text.' Yet this did not alter, could not alter, the deep-seated, internal 'operating system' that had been placed there by the Lord. That 'operating system', if you will, ran all the programs for Paul. The grace of God that would cause Paul in 1 Timothy 1:2-16 to explain to Pastor Timothy that the way to deal with all the extensive challenges in Ephesus was to minister out of the sacred encounter and divine calling that one has with and from the risen Lord Jesus Christ, is what also led to the spontaneous doxological combustion in verse 17: 'Now to the King eternal, immortal, invisible, to God who alone is wise, be honor and glory forever and ever. Amen.'

Thus, the internal operating system, his conversion, leads to a constant expression of praise. He ministers out of a core that is a veritable nuclear reactor of grace that produces a life of praise, whether in prison or being beaten or ministering freely before pagan philosophers on Mars Hill. This is the 'one-sermon' motif that ruled his life. God's grace can save anyone, anywhere, with any past. Paul's own life had become 'a pattern to those who are going to believe on him for everlasting life' (1 Tim. 1:16).

What is your one sermon? If you are a believer you have one. If you are a believer who has been called to preach the unsearchable riches of Christ to others, then you surely have one. Your one sermon is what God has done in your life. Your one sermon is your sacred encounter. It is your divine calling. It may be the one sermon of a faithful covenant family who were used of God to bring you to Christ in the home with godly examples. Your calling to preach came as you realized the brokenness of the world which did not have that experience. Or, it may be the sacred encounter of Christ in a prison cell and then the wrestling you had when you knew God was calling you to preach, like Charles Colson, to other prisoners, whether bound in the shackles of a penitentiary or the chains of false religion. That is your one sermon. John Wesley was a 'brand plucked from the burning' and that theme runs throughout all his messages. George Whitefield burned alive with the glory of his assurance of salvation. Can you read Whitefield and not come away with that one sermon? C.H. Spurgeon was arrested by the lay preacher who called for him to 'look, look!' and to see his salvation in the Lord. He would call many others to 'look' to God in thousands of messages, strong with that one compelling mandate which became his one sermon.

What is your one sermon? What makes you burn alive with Christ until your messages break out in a holy conflagration of praise? That 'one sermon' is the work of God in you and it will be the Spirit-compelling feature of your ministry which will cause you to preach every sermon, from every text, with gospel power and scriptural faithfulness.

I, therefore, appeal to you now: bring all of your studies to the bar of God, recalling His work in your life, His call on your life, and go to preach one sermon for the rest of your life. And others will break into spontaneous doxological combustion too.

In the name of the Father, and of the Son, and of the Holy Spirit.

In Christ,
Mike Milton.

❧ 19 ❧

THE GROUND OF YOUR MINISTRY

Our Dear Students,

I write to you now about ways of approaching your ministry. Here's a question for you: Is it a 'practical theology' that is primarily aimed at 'how to' or is it a 'pastoral theology' grounded in the Biblical-theological truths of the Reformation? I want to caution you to think about this carefully. Your perspective will determine the character and lasting impact (or temporary impression) of your ministerial career. I would say that the answer to this question should also determine whether you are a candidate for burnout in the ministry, whether you have the strength to run the race of faith in the ministry, and how you will deal with both success and disappointment in the pastoral ministry. In short, the answer to the question will provide the over-arching and all encompassing way as to how you will conduct your ministry.

Martin Bucer (1491-1551) is helpful in answering this question. This pastor-scholar, a 'reformer in the wings' as Andrew Purves refers to him, said that all pastoral ministries must be 'rooted directly in biblical and Reformational faith and ... oriented to the practical care of souls.'[1] Bucer was a great churchman, pastor at Strasbourg, a teacher of Calvin, a framer of Reformed worship, a contributor to the Book of Common Prayer (1552) and an esteemed professor of theology at Cambridge. (His body was exhumed by Queen Mary four years after his death to be burned in public, only to be 'restored to full honor' five years later by Elizabeth I.) Bucer taught that the warrant, the calling and the work of the pastor, must be grounded in the Word of God and in the theological commitments of the Reformation, and must be embraced personally by the pastor. In other words, the pastoral ministry is not only a biblical idea, though it must be so; it is also a Spirit-shaped reality in the soul of the one called to be a pastor.

After I came to the end of my wrestling, or so I thought, to follow the call to the ordained ministry, I visited my dear Aunt Eva in Kansas. While there, the chaplain of her nursing home came and spoke with me. Dr Eckley himself was a man of about ninety years of age. But he ministered to the residents there with the energy and seriousness and pastoral care that had marked his long career as a Nazarene pastor, district superintendent, and missionary.

'Mike,' he began with a kindly smile, 'I heard that you are going to seminary.' I told him that I was. He drew closer to me, eyeball to eyeball. 'Son, I have one question for you: Are you really called by God to shepherd His flock?' I paused. I drew

---

1. See Martin Bucer (rpt 2009), *Concerning the True Care of Souls*, Banner of Truth.

back a little and gathered myself together before I answered. I was careful in my words. 'Dr Eckley, I think so.'

His eyes became like flames at my answer. 'Well, son, you are not ready to follow the Lord.' I was dumbstruck. 'Boy, if you only *think* that you are called, then you will fall. You had better know that God has laid His hand upon you. You had better know His holy call in your soul. You need to know what God says about pastors in His Word and the great burden of souls that a minister will bear all of the days of his life. I tell you this, son, because when the winds of hardship blow your way you will only have one thing. Do you know what that is?'

I hesitated to break up the private sermon he was giving me but I felt I should answer. 'The call?' 'Yes! You only have your call from God! When they give you a Christmas raise and then run you out on a rumor, when the devil stirs up opposition against you for the sake of Jesus, and when you are hurt like our Lord was hurt, you will only have one thing to help you pick up your things and move on to the next field of service. Do you know what that is?' I decided not to answer. 'You know what it is? It is your calling from God.'

We both stood there looking at each other without talking. This eternity lasted for about a minute. Then he laid down the hammer for the final time. 'Son, are you called by God to be a pastor according to the Word of God?' I whispered that I thought I should go home and pray about it.

Brothers, I went and did so. I reviewed again what God's Word said. I came face to face with the weight of the ministry as well as the unbelievable joy that must also be in it. I realized that God was calling even me to preach the unsearchable riches of Jesus Christ our Lord. That calling has never left me to this day. I went back and told Dr Eckley that I now could answer his question. 'By God's grace, I am called and am ready to take up the cross if he will help me.' 'Good,' the old Wesleyan said to the Calvinist. 'Good, Mike. Go and preach the gospel. Go to seminary and learn what it is that will ground you in the ministry of the gospel for the rest of your life.'

I write to encourage you to see that in every class you take at this seminary you are tethering your life to the biblical and theological rock that will guide you in every area of ministry for the rest of your life. Do not neglect your Greek. You will have to exegete and exposit the words of Paul and Luke and Peter for the blood-bought lambs of Jesus. Do not learn your Hebrew verb forms only to pass a test, but to stand the test, the test of pastoral ministry. You have been called to stand between God and men and women and boys and girls with God's Word. From the Bible give the gospel bread of life to your people living in your city in your generation.

Don't skim over the readings from church history. Identify your life with Bucer and Luther and Baxter and Machen. Prayerfully study the providential ways of God in the Patristic period as well as in the Reformation period. How will that shape your leadership of God's people today? As you listen to teaching on perichoresis and Holy Trinity and God's immanence and His transcendence, do not think that this is far from how you will minister God's love in the midst of the community of God's people. In short, my dearest ones in Christ, you must embrace every opportunity here to prepare your heart and mind to minister the glorious gospel of God's Son to a dying world and to shepherd the saints of Christ.

The 'how to' of ministry must begin with the God of the Bible. The pastoral ministry finds its warrant and its vocational vision from God's Word. You will never be vocationally and spiritually satisfied with anything short of a Christ-centered ministry because it is God who calls you. Burnout and pride and apostasy will lurk in the shadows of your ministry like hungry wolves, or more Scripturally put, like a roaring lion seeking whom he may devour. But a pastoral theology grounded in the Word and the ordinary means of grace – Word, sacrament, and prayer – will surround you and protect you and lead you forward to the crown that God has prepared for those who serve Him to the end.

I am thinking on these things this morning. I am asking God to give you a ministry of the Word that will endure and bring about transformation of hearts and minds, of cultures and entire generations, so that a multitude will be 'safe in the arms of Jesus' when He comes again (1 Thess. 2:19-20). And so I write these words to stir your thoughts and to encourage you.

Yours in Christ,
Mike Milton.

❧20❧

SUNDAY NIGHT REST

My dear brothers and sisters in Christ,

I want to write to you about the practical application of a very important text for your lives: 'And he said to them, "Come away by yourselves to a desolate place and rest a while." For many were coming and going, and they had no leisure even to eat' (Mark 6:31). 'Many were coming and going.' That is the happy disposition of our work and it is also the very thing that brings us much weariness.

I have always loved Sundays as a pastor. It is the culmination of a week of ministry for Christ. During the week I might have held the hands of family members in vigil as death approached their loved one. I might have gone from that hospital room to prepare for a wedding on the coming Saturday afternoon. There would have been the last counseling session, followed by the Friday night rehearsal during which I would have received the predictable charge by the bride's mother, or another family member, about this or that detail, the also predictable but uneasy talk with their wedding coordinator, and finally my own presentation of the gospel to the family which would make it all worthwhile.

In the middle of that week I might have had a session meeting, followed the next day by an early morning Bible study. This meant, of course, that after the session meeting, which would have lasted too long because one of the elders was upset about the budget or the lack of sympathy for his theological conviction in the Sunday School curriculum (though he didn't put it that way), I would have had to spend late hours preparing for the pre-dawn study on Romans. Into that soup of pastoral activities might have been added staff meetings, committee meetings, a Rotary luncheon, and scheduled and spontaneous counseling times.

Of course my family would need me too! My son might have had a wrestling match or a Boy Scout meeting and I would not have wanted to be a proverbial absentee father always caring for others in the flock to the neglect of my own family.

But through it all, in it all, and under it all, there would have been the preparation of the message. There would have been prayer. I would have long before created a sermon planner, so I would know where I was going. On Monday I would have read the text, laid it out, perhaps even discovered the expository rhythms to the passage. By Thursday I would have understood, through prayer and time with the Lord in the hospital room and nursing home, as well as in the study, the outline I would use to help others receive the message. And sometime before I would have prepared the wedding sermon, I would have written the message in manuscript form as I almost always do. On Saturday night, I would have read the manuscript to my family as a devotion and for their responses. We would have sealed it with prayer.

And that night, as on every Saturday night, I would have skimmed over sleep, reciting the outline in my mind, dealing with the introductory chain, identifying the main proposition, moving through the transitional phrases, and finally examining my concluding statements. Then, when sleep would have finally come at around 5:30 AM, the alarm would go off. I would then have dashed from the bathroom to the clothes closet to the study. The things that God gave me in the night would have merged with the work from the week, and the message would have been steeped from the times in Bible study, wrestling match, counseling, wedding and cutting the grass. And the sermon would be ready. Off I would go to the early service, the first prayer meeting with officers, and the Sunday School, along with meeting and greeting and counseling.

But the moment that I longed for every week would have come when I stepped into the pulpit and said, 'This is the day that the Lord has made, we will rejoice and be glad in it!' And off I would have gone into leading the worship. And then to open up the Word of God and begin to preach that which I was burdened with was such a joy. To preach the message and look across and see the faces and know the stories of God's grace that I would have heard as their pastor is one of the great joys of pastoral ministry in this life.

But it all takes a toll. And if you have Sunday night worship and you are preaching again, though the rhythms of that service are quite different, it is still a labor of love that will zap your strength. Indeed, at the end of Sunday, the end of your week, 'many were coming and going.' But there in that place of exhaustion, when the week's ministry is behind you, and tomorrow's challenges have not yet come, there can be a most glorious and exhilarating time when you hear the Master bid you: 'Come away by yourselves to a desolate place and rest a while.' In the week-to-week cycle of ministry, Sunday nights from 8:00 until 10:30 were the 'desolate place' for my family and me. Here the Lord met with us and brought succor and healing.

I am thinking of these things and I am praying that you will find that desolate place in your life as a seminarian now. Come away with Jesus for a while. There will be much work to do tomorrow. And you have labored well today. Unless you find Him in the quiet places of your life, you might lose your way. Listen to His voice. Follow His loving command. Come away for a while.

I commend you to Christ and to the Word of his grace,

Mike Milton.

But people no longer write letters. Lacking the leisure and for the most part, the ability, they dictate dispatches and scribble messages. When you are in the humor, you should take a peep at some of the letters written by people who lived long ago, especially the letters of women. There is a charm about them impossible to describe, the charm of unconsciousness and the sweetness of real sincerity. But in these days, we have neither the artfulness nor the freedom of our forebears. We know too little about ourselves. Constraint covers us like a curtain. Not being very sure of our feelings, we are in a fog about the feelings of others.

— Joel Chandler Harris (1848-1908)
letter to his son, April 5, 1900.

CONCLUSION

Thank you for reading. As I reflect on the matter of writing as a way of teaching theology (and the practice of pastoral ministry), I am more convinced than ever that the most effective method of transmitting knowledge of God and this calling is, of necessity, through relationship. A letter helps to support that relationship.

As we close, I would point you to a few of my favorite books in this genre: theology through letters. While not expressly written for pastors, these choice selections make a compelling case for returning to the art of thinking, dreaming, and, yes, even shepherding the flock of God through the medium of correspondence.

What if you, too, joined the cloud of witnesses gone before – including the prophets, apostles, and great saints of the ages – and wrote pastoral letters to your fellow disciples, or your family? Or *just* to your wife or to your husband? I believe that you would deposit a jewel of inestimable value into the archives of time, one demonstrating that rare, but loveliest of virtues: thinking thoughts about God within a relationship with another person.

Here are some books for you to enjoy.

Houston, James M. *Letters of Faith through the Seasons: A Treasury of Great Christians' Correspondence.* Colorado

Springs, CO: Honor Books, 2007. 'If you were to have one book on letters...' Yes, this would be the one for me. James Houston is the personification of this literate way of thinking theologically through letters. The book is an anthology. I love this book because the always trustworthy Dr Houston takes us on a journey with great Christian letter-writers, pastors and non-clergy alike. Moreover, the letters are thoughtfully (and, no doubt, painstakingly) placed by the author within the helpful order of the Christian Year. From Advent (the season I live in as I write) I read, 'Ultimately, all our seasonal circumstances have to be faced in the reality of our heavenly destiny. There only will all be all and in all. The spring may express the beauty of the Christian life, while the autumn may bring forth joy. So what then of the winter? The winter is needed to exercise self-denial, and to exercise in a thousand small ways the struggles we go through to live devotionally. It is a climate of spiritual dryness, perhaps, yet little by little we endure it, provided we have godliness and are determined not to get discouraged, but persist in the fortitude of faith ... Let us then live joyously and courageously, my dear daughter. There is absolutely no doubt whatsoever of the reality that Jesus Christ is our life.' This particular letter, a rich source of pastoral thought, is from Francis de Sales (1567-1622), Catholic Bishop of Geneva, in his correspondence, on February 11, 1607, to Madame de Chantal. Enriched will be the pastor, student, academic, or disciple of any vocation, who thinks through the year with this wise collection.

Lewis, C.S. *The Screwtape Letters*. San Francisco: HarperSanFrancisco, 2001. This is one of the most notable examples of theology delivered through letter. And one of the most thoughtful, provocative, and creative.

Lewis, C.S., and Clyde S. Kilby. *Letters to an American Lady*. Grand Rapids, MI: W.B. Eerdmans Pub., 1967.

Lewis, C.S., and Walter Hooper. *The Collected Letters of C.S. Lewis*. San Francisco: HarperSanFrancisco, 2004.

Lewis, C.S., Arthur Greeves, and Walter Hooper. *They Stand Together: The Letters of C.S. Lewis to Arthur Greeves, 1914-1963*. New York: Macmillan Pub., 1979.

Lewis, C.S. *Letters to Malcolm: Chiefly on Prayer*. New York: Harcourt, Brace & World, 1964. In my own spiritual awakening, I remember reading Lewis on prayer and drinking the theological nectar drawn from the fruit of this book. Wonderful and timeless.

Lewis, C.S., Lyle W. Dorsett, and Marjorie Lamp Mead. *C.S. Lewis Letters to Children*. New York: Macmillan, 1985. You have, perhaps, seen quotes from this book. This fine collection expresses the cherished spiritual tradition of thinking theologically within the context of communication with children. No one did it better than Lewis.

Miller, Samuel, and Presbyterian Church in the U.S.A. (Old School) Board of Publication. *Letters on Clerical Manners and Habits: Addressed to a Student in the Theological Seminary, at Princeton, N.J.* Philadelphia: Presbyterian Board of Publication, 1852. The concept of writing on pastoral theology to seminary students is not new. Dr Samuel Miller of Princeton wrote many such letters. Some were collected, like my own, and put into print. The result. A wonderful compilation of thought on the seminary life and practical training for ministry. Some of his thoughts, about how to come to a lecture, for instance, might seem dated, but I maintain there is something to take from them for all time. E.g., 'Never allow yourself to enter the lecture room in a slovenly dress' (20). Anachronistic? Or timeless?

Pascal, Blaise, W.F. Trotter, and Thomas M'Crie. *Pensées: The Provincial Letters*. New York: Modern Library, 1941. This is not a book of 'pure' correspondence, but rather, as the title suggests, the 'thoughts' of the great thinker. Yet these fragments from his life belong to this genre of literature: reflective, personal, intimate in tone; and, yet, extraordinarily theological in nature. Consider this insight: 'The only thing which consoles us for our miseries is diversion, and yet this is the greatest of our miseries. For it is this which principally hinders us from reflecting upon ourselves and which makes us insensibly ruin ourselves' (From Section One: Thoughts on Mind and Style).

Wayland, Francis. *Letters on the Ministry of the Gospel.* Boston: Gould and Lincoln, 1863. Francis Wayland (March 11, 1796–September 30, 1865) was a remarkable American Baptist minister. He was the fourth president of Brown University, one of the founders of Andover Newton Theological Seminary, and a vociferous temperance and anti-slavery advocate, whose vision became a reality in a new seminary for those Americans of African descent. Named in his honor, the former Wayland Seminary has now become Virginia Union Seminary. This is an extraordinary book by Dr Wayland, demonstrating his razor-sharp mind and devotion to an educated ministry and, yet, one that is altogether committed to supernatural power. Thus, in letter three, he writes to students on why ministry is not a profession. This is not only fascinating, but – at least I experienced – vocationally nourishing reading for the pastor.

Other books of interest from

Christian Focus Publications

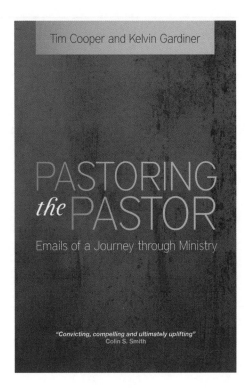

Tim Cooper and Kelvin Gardiner

PASTORING
the PASTOR

Emails of a Journey through Ministry

"Convicting, compelling and ultimately uplifting"
Colin S. Smith

ISBN 978-1-84550-784-8

Pastoring the Pastor

Emails of a Journey through Ministry

TIM COOPER AND KELVIN GARDINER

Daniel Donford is a new pastor: excited, filled with bright dreams, anticipating a big future for him and his new church, Broadfield Community Church. However opposition and obstacles lie just ahead, and both may end his journey into pastoral ministry before it has really begun. But Dan has an Uncle Eldon, if anyone can see Dan through his trials and disasters, Eldon can. The wisdom he offers, via a series of emails, might just be enough to see Dan transformed into the mature, selfless, loving pastor God wants him to be.

> Convicting, compelling and ultimately uplifting; this insightful probing of the realities of pastoral ministry will make you smile, lead you to pray, and encourage you to persevere.
>
> Colin S. Smith,
> Senior Pastor, The Orchard Evangelical Free Church, Arlington, Illinois

> I plan to commend this book to our students here at Beeson Divinity School and to pastors everywhere who are called to the burdensome joy of shepherding the flock of God.
>
> Timothy George,
> Founding Dean of Beeson Divinity School,
> Samford University, Birmingham, Alabama

> I could scarcely put this book down as I relived the pitfalls and missteps of the early days of pastoral ministry, but then the glories of wisdom, perseverance, and hope that gradually emerges. No matter what your pastoral setting, this book will help you get – or stay – on the paths of righteousness.
>
> Greg Scharf,
> Chair of the Pastoral Theology Department and Professor of Pastoral Theology,
> Trinity Evangelical Divinity School, Deerfield, Illinois

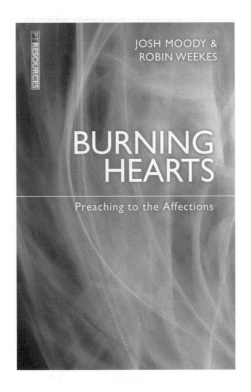

JOSH MOODY &
ROBIN WEEKES

PT RESOURCES

BURNING
HEARTS

Preaching to the Affections

ISBN 978-1-78191-403-8

Burning Hearts

Preaching to the Affections

JOSH MOODY AND ROBIN WEEKES

Affection is often a neglected theme in our generation of Bible believing Christians. It has not always been so. Previous generations thought a great deal about the centrality of the heart in the Christian life and the need to preach to it. This book will prove a valuable resource as we learn about the place of the affections in our walk with Christ and in preaching Him to ourselves and others.

> For some, this little book will be a healthy reminder; for others, it will revolutionize their preaching.
>
> **D. A. Carson,**
> Research Professor of New Testament,
> Trinity Evangelical Divinity School, Deerfield, Illinois

> It has not only convinced me of the importance of preaching to the affections, but has also inspired me to think that I must and can do this better.
>
> **Vaughan Roberts,**
> Rector of St Ebbe's, Oxford and Director of Proclamation Trust

> Messrs Moody & Weekes, with plenty of good sense, would encourage us preachers to reach the hearts of our listeners... Are they making a timely point? I think they are.
>
> **Dick Lucas,**
> Formerly Rector of St Helen's Bishopsgate, London

> This book turns on the lights, helping preachers understand how hearts and lives can be affected by truth. I'm thrilled to see this book, handling such an important subject so well.
>
> **Michael Reeves,**
> Theologian at Large, Wales Evangelical School of Theology, Bridgend, Wales

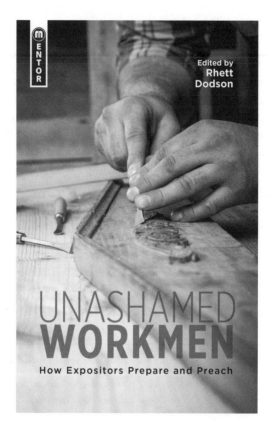

UNASHAMED
WORKMEN
How Expositors Prepare and Preach

Edited by
**Rhett
Dodson**

ISBN 978-1-78191-319-2

Unashamed Workmen

How Expositors Prepare and Preach

EDITED BY RHETT DODSON

Bringing together some of the finest preachers of our day, *Unashamed Workmen* focuses on the methods they use to prepare their sermons. You will find a variety of approaches and styles but they all share a passion for the Word of God to be explained and applied clearly.

Contributors:
Peter Adam, Rhett Dodson, Iain Duguid, Ajith Fernando, David Jackman, Simon Manchester, David Meredith, Josh Moody, Douglas Sean O'Donnell Richard D Phillips.

This is a great book. It brings together diverse and complementary voices from experienced expository preachers who are thoroughly committed to the Gospel. It is not a textbook. Its strength and freshness depend on the sweep of voices.

D. A. Carson,
Research Professor of New Testament,
Trinity Evangelical Divinity School, Deerfield, Illinois

Unashamed Workmen is like looking into the mind and over the shoulder of ten master expositors as they prepare, and then sitting in the audience as they deliver the fruits of their labours.

Hershael W. York,
Victor & Louise Lester Professor of Preaching,
The Southern Baptist Theological Seminary, Louisville, Kentucky

...a tour of the workshops of talented preachers, enabling us to look over the shoulders of these master craftsmen of proclaimed truth in order to learn how we might produce messages reflecting the beauty and utility of their sermons.

Bryan Chapell,
Pastor, Grace Presbyterian Church, Peoria, Illinois

ALEC MOTYER

PREACHING?

Simple Teaching on Simply Preaching

"Alec Motyer has had a profound, formative influence on
my preaching. In this book he puts his decades of wisdom on
expository preaching at the reader's fingertips" Tim Keller

ISBN 978-1-78191-130-3

Preaching?

Simple Teaching on Simply Preaching

ALEC MOTYER

Like many things in life, the skill of good preaching is 95% perspiration and 5% inspiration. Alec Motyer's guide is based on a multitude of sermons over many years of preaching in many different situations, a recipe to help you know your subject and to pull the pieces together into a winning sermon. Preaching is a privilege: let Alec help you reach out and make the best of the gifts God has given you.

> Alec Motyer has had a profound, formative influence on my preaching. In this book he puts his decades of wisdom on expository preaching at the reader's fingertips. This is as practical and Biblically solid a book on preaching as you can find today.
>
> Tim Keller,
> Senior Pastor, Redeemer Presbyterian Church, New York City, New York

> Given the content, readability and insights... this book is a "must" for preachers and for those who want to understand preaching and encourage preachers.
>
> Harry Reeder,
> Pastor of Preaching & Leadership,
> Briarwood Presbyterian Church, Birmingham, Alabama

> Alec's succinct and stirring treatise on preaching makes me wish wholeheartedly that I could start all over again-in that blessed privilege of preaching, praying and pastoring..
>
> Dale Ralph Davis,
> Minister in Residence, First Presbyterian Church, Columbia, South Carolina

> This refreshing guide, laced with excellent Biblical examples and astute observations from personal experience, will be a great read for preachers old and new, and I warmly commend it.
>
> Jonathan Lamb,
> Keswick Ministries, CEO and minister-at-large

Christian Focus Publications

Our mission statement –

STAYING FAITHFUL
In dependence upon God we seek to impact the world through literature faithful to His infallible Word, the Bible. Our aim is to ensure that the Lord Jesus Christ is presented as the only hope to obtain forgiveness of sin, live a useful life and look forward to heaven with Him.

Our books are published in four imprints:

CHRISTIAN
FOCUS

Popular works including biographies, commentaries, basic doctrine and Christian living.

CHRISTIAN
HERITAGE

Books representing some of the best material from the rich heritage of the church.

MENTOR

Books written at a level suitable for Bible College and seminary students, pastors, and other serious readers. The imprint includes commentaries, doctrinal studies, examination of current issues and church history.

CF4•K

Children's books for quality Bible teaching and for all age groups: Sunday school curriculum, puzzle and activity books; personal and family devotional titles, biographies and inspirational stories – Because you are never too young to know Jesus!

Christian Focus Publications Ltd,
Geanies House, Fearn, Ross-shire,
IV20 1TW, Scotland, United Kingdom
www.christianfocus.com